Discover!
Social Studies

3

Discover! Social Studies 3B

Published in Catasauqua, Pennsylvania by Discover Press, a division of Edovate Learning Corp.

334 2nd Street

Catasauqua, PA 18032

edovate.com

ISBN: 978-1-956330-07-6

Printed in United States of America

1st Edition

Table of Contents

Worktexts & Instructor Guides

Worktexts

- Your Discover! course integrates all reading, writing, practice, ideas to extend learning, and opportunities for students to capture their ideas and connect learning to what matters to them.

- By providing both direct instruction and assessment opportunities, students are able to gain knowledge, reflect on what they learned, and apply it in both academic and real-world environments.

- To meet the needs of all learners, each worktext includes activities, instruction, and extensions that appeal to all learning styles.

- Each chapter is made up of lessons that connect to a central theme. Students have the opportunity to demonstrate understanding and think critically as they move through each lesson, and each chapter culminates with a student review, assessment, and opportunities for students to show what they know.

Instructor Guides

- Each instructor guide is specifically constructed to complement the worktext, provide helpful suggestions for a home-based instructor, offer support, and broaden a student's knowledge base.

- Instruction and curriculum are differentiated with remediation, enrichment, assessment, and supporting activities suitable for a variety of learning styles.

- Answer keys for all activities are included in your instructor guide.

Planning Your Day & School Year

- Each lesson takes approximately two to three days to complete, for a total of around 150 days of instruction through the school year. NOTE: Your worktext and instructor guide provide enrichment activities and discussion questions to take learning further and may add extra days to the school year. These are designed to inspire the instructor to customize the learning experience even further and encourage students to dive deeper into the topic.

- As you begin each lesson, we recommend completing three pages on the first day and two pages, including Show What You Know, on the second day.

- In the chapter reviews and assessment lessons, we recommend completing three pages on the first day and the remaining pages on the second day.

Parts of a Lesson

Lesson Overview (PAGE 1):

Each lesson opens with a list of goals or objectives designed to set the student up for success. Your instructor guide provides additional resources to reinforce concepts and add creativity to the lesson.

Explore (PAGE 2):

This page is key, as it is designed to engage students and encourage the discovery of new concepts.

Direct Instruction (PAGES 3–5):

In this section, the student gets to work by reading the content, capturing their own thoughts and ideas, and then practicing the concepts:

- **Read**: Students read informational text to gain knowledge about the lesson topic.
- **Write**: Students reflect on what they have read by creating a written response.
- **Practice**: Students practice what they have learned through various engaging activities, such as graphic organizers, matching, drawing, experiments, and hands-on learning.

Show What You Know (PAGE 6):

This is where students demonstrate what they've learned by completing a carefully crafted assessment aligned with the lesson's objectives.

To reinforce learning, additional extension activities are included throughout each lesson:

- **Create**: Students are tasked with constructing a piece of art, such as a drawing, song, poem, model, etc., to demonstrate learning.
- **Take a Closer Look**: With these activities, students make observations about the world around them. In doing so, students are able to generate predictions, inferences, or conclusions based on those observations. In science, these are scientific investigations or STEM-based activities.
- **In the Real World**: These activities connect the lesson to real-world situations. Students get the opportunity to investigate or interact with real-world examples.
- **Online Connection**: Students use technology-based solutions to research and investigate concepts related to the lesson or create artifacts demonstrating their understanding.
- **Play**: In these activities, students create or play games related to the lesson, such as board games, card games, role-playing, etc.

Chapter 9
International Relationships

Hi there! It is Julia! The coolest grasshopper in Texas.

We got back to Texas and brought more corn with us. Everyone in the grasslands was happy. Now we had wheat and corn. Our neighbors ate better. We were all healthier. Even Ms. Cricket was less annoying now!

But then we got a phone call from our cousins in Mexico. The President of the country announced they would not buy any more wheat from the United States. The American president was angry. So he said we would not buy corn from Mexico!

Do you want to hear what happened next? Be ready, young grasshopper!

Fights are never good. When I fight with my brother and sister, my mom forces us to make up. But what happens when countries fight? Where do they go?

Fun fact: There is a building in New York City. It is called the United Nations building. That is where countries go to settle their fights.

My mom had an idea. We should go to New York and bring our cousins from Acapulco. Then we will tell the world how much better it is when we get along.

I went to pack my bags. I have never been to New York City! But I am always ready for a new adventure. So let's hop to it!

What Will I Learn?

This chapter looks at international relations. It focuses on what drives different states apart and how they work together to resolve conflicts.

Lessons at a Glance

Lesson 36

Forms of Government

By the end of this lesson, you will be able to:

- explain that different nations have different forms of government

Lesson Review

If you need to review government, please go to the lesson titled "Government Around the World" or "National Governments."

Academic Vocabulary

Read the following vocabulary words and definitions. Look through the lesson. Can you find each vocabulary word? Underline the vocabulary word in your lesson. Write the page number of where you found each word in the blanks.

- **aristocracy:** a type of government where the highest class holds power over the lower class (page ____)
- **constitution:** a document that contains the rules of a country or organization (page ____)
- **democracy:** a type of government ruled by the citizens (page ____)
- **government:** a group with the power to make and carry out laws (page ____)
- **monarchy:** a type of government ruled by a single crowned leader (page ____)
- **oligarchy:** a type of government ruled by a small group of powerful people (page ____)

Think about the country you live in. Who is the leader? Perhaps you have a queen, a president, or an emperor. Consider what you know of the government in your country. Can you identify how the leader of your country came to be in power? Make a list of questions you might have about your leader. Think about who the leader is and what they do to lead the country. Discuss your questions with your instructor.

EXPLORE

Imagine you have the power to build a nation. You find an island and declare it a brand-new country. To run your country, you will need to form a national government. This will help things run smoothly. Complete the chart to start planning out your government:

Nation Name: What will you call your country?	**National Leader:** Who will be the leader?
National Flag: What will the flag look like?	**National Motto:** What is your country's tagline?
Laws: Who do you want to be in charge of writing laws for your country?	**Military:** Who do you want to be in charge of your country's defense?
Rules: What is one of the rules you would have in your country?	**Consequences:** What happens if you break the rules or laws of your country?

IN THE REAL WORLD

Name the Leader

There have been lots of different types of leaders throughout history and all sorts of names to go with them! Check out a few of them below. How many of these have you heard of?

- King and Queen
- President
- Pope
- Emperor
- Maharaja
- Sultan
- Chief
- Czar

READ

World Leaders

Our world is made up of about 195 countries, and each of them is run by a government. A **government** is a group of leaders who make decisions and rules for a community or country. How a government works varies from country to country. The forms of government are defined by its leaders. In most countries, leaders are chosen in one of two ways:

ELECTIONS

Elected leaders are chosen by the citizens of the country in a process called voting. During an election, all citizens who are allowed to vote can choose which person they think should win. Whoever gets the most votes wins and gets the job until the next election.

Elections have a lot of rules to keep things fair. For example, cities and counties get to decide who is eligible to run for office based on things like age, where they live, how long they have lived there, and other criteria.

ROYAL SUCCESSION

Some leaders come to power by being part of a royal family. Leadership is passed from generation to generation. There are often strict guidelines for determining the heir to the throne, especially when a king or queen dies without children. In the past, there have also been rules against women being heirs to the throne.

Sometimes people fought over who was the rightful heir to the crown. Sometimes an outsider would come in and defeat the kingdom in battle, force the king or queen off the throne, and take over.

WRITE   Do you believe election or royal succession is a better way of choosing leaders? Explain which you think is better and why.

....

....

....

....

Forms of Government

Different nations organize their governments in different ways.

Read more about each type of government and its leaders below. As you read, underline any key words or phrases you feel are important to the form of government.

 **DEMOCRACY**	A **democracy** is a type of government ruled by the citizens. It is up to the nation's citizens to vote for their leader. The goal of a democracy is to have fair representation within the government. A democracy makes sure the people in charge are good leaders and are not abusing their power.
MONARCHY	In a **monarchy**, a single leader holds power. The leader is usually a king, a queen, or an emperor. Leaders in a monarchy are handed power through their family bloodline. Some countries with a monarch are still run as a democracy, so the citizens have power to vote and change government policies.
 **OLIGARCHY**	In an **oligarchy**, a small group of leaders holds the power. Wealth, heredity, and race are factors used to give all the power to those leaders. Leaders usually gain control with money or military strength. Oligarchies do not allow voting, so the citizens do not have a say in what happens. Leaders typically do not care about fairness or citizens' rights.
 **ARISTOCRACY**	An **aristocracy** is a government where the wealthy upper class have power over those with less money and status. Leaders in an aristocracy are chosen based on their wealth, education, or family status. The rules and policies are chosen to benefit only the aristocrats and typically leave the lower class without any say.

PRACTICE

Read the following descriptions about the systems of government in four different countries. As you read, circle any key words or phrases that might hint toward which type is used. Can you identify the type of government in each of these countries? Talk about your ideas with your instructor.

New Zealand does have a queen, but the government is run by elected leaders too. Citizens can vote to elect the leaders of their choice.

Saudi Arabia is ruled by a king. The king is in charge of making all the rules. When the current king dies, the throne is passed down to his son.

Myanmar is under military control. Leaders of the military took control from the elected leaders. The leader of the armed forces is now the leader of the country.

The president of **Turkey** is an elected position. Some leaders are voted in by the citizens, and some by members of the government. One very powerful family controls most of the money in Turkey.

REVIEW

In this lesson, you learned:

- World leaders come to power through elections or royal bloodlines.

- The four main forms of government are democracy, monarchy, oligarchy, and aristocracy.

- Different nations practice different forms of government.

Think About It

Think about the four main government systems of democracy, monarchy, oligarchy, and aristocracy. Reflect on the possible pros and cons of each type. Consider how you would run a country if you were its leader. Which type of government would you prefer to rule?

SHOW WHAT YOU KNOW

Read each sentence. Circle True or False.

1. True or False   Every country has the same type of government.

2. True or False   Leaders are chosen through votes during an election.

3. True or False   Leaders can pass the crown through a family bloodline.

4. True or False   A monarchy is a government run by one person.

5. True or False   An aristocracy benefits both the rich and the poor.

6. True or False   People vote in elections in a democracy.

Match each situation to the type of government being described.

7. _____ aristocracy

8. _____ oligarchy

9. _____ democracy

10. _____ monarchy

A. A king reigns. When he dies, his crown will be passed onto his eldest daughter. She will be the new queen.

B. There were two choices for leader, but one got more people to vote for them. That is how they were chosen to lead.

C. A small group of people have so much money and power that they have forced control of the government.

D. Those with wealth and elite status create rules that benefit their families. The poor families stay poor while the rich families get richer.

ONLINE CONNECTION

Go online to learn more about the government in your area. Research information on the following:

- the form of government in your country
- the national leader of your country
- how your national leader came to power
- the local leaders of your city and state
- how your local leaders came to power

Discuss your findings with your instructor.

Leaders of the World

By the end of this lesson, you will be able to:

- describe the role of world leaders
- explain how world leaders interact with each other

Lesson Review

If you need to review government, please go to the lesson titled "Government Around the World."

Academic Vocabulary

Read the following vocabulary words and definitions. Look through the lesson. Can you find each vocabulary word? Underline the vocabulary word in your lesson. Write the page number of where you found each word in the blanks.

- **chief of state:** the highest leader in a country (page ____)
- **domestic policy:** developing solutions for challenges within one's own country (page ____)
- **foreign policy:** developing solutions and ways of working with other countries (page ____)
- **leader:** the person in charge of a group (page ____)
- **world leader:** the leader of an entire country (page____)

CREATE

Draw a picture of yourself as the leader of a country. What would you wear? Where would you work?

Once you are finished the lesson, look back at the picture you drew of yourself as the leader of a country. What does it take to be a good world leader? What kind of leader would you want to be? Add some adjectives to your picture to describe what type of leader you would want to be.

Think about leaders in your life. Maybe you play a team sport like soccer. The soccer coach is the **leader**, or person in charge, of the team. They are in charge of keeping players safe, resolving arguments, encouraging fair play, and guiding your team to win games.

What if your coach was really mean or unfair? Would you still want to be part of a team with a bad leader? No! It is important for leaders to have character traits that inspire the team to succeed. These character traits are called *leadership qualities*. Here are some qualities of a good leader:

L—listen: Good leaders listen to people's ideas.

E—encourage: Good leaders encourage those they work with.

A—appreciate: Leaders need to show that they appreciate others.

D—deliver: Good leaders do the things they say they will do.

Think of a few leaders you know, like a coach, dance instructor, youth pastor, or parent, who shows good leadership qualities. What makes them a good leader?

Discuss your ideas with your instructor.

IN THE REAL WORLD

In professional soccer, the team is led by a captain. One of the greatest captains of all time was Paolo Maldini, a leader of AC Milan and the Italian national team. He led the team to win many matches and was such a great leader that his nickname was Il Capitano, which means "The Captain" in Italian. He inspired his teammates with his style of play, dedication to the team, and commitment to AC Milan.

READ

What Is a World Leader?

When someone is the leader of an entire country, they are considered a **world leader**. Being a world leader comes with a lot of power and responsibility. World leaders have to lead the citizens of their country, but they also represent their country to the rest of the world. Leaders of small countries hold less power than leaders of large countries. The more power a country has in the world, the more influence their leader has on global issues.

LEADING THE COUNTRY

The leader of a government is called the **chief of state**. The chief of state has many jobs within their own country. The chief of state must symbolically represent the citizens. They work hard to execute, create, and change laws. They are in charge of the military. When the chief of state develops solutions for challenges within their country, it is called **domestic policy**.

LEADING IN THE WORLD

The chief of state also represents their country to the rest of the world. World leaders come together to manage conflict at a global level. If there is something affecting the whole planet, the world leaders will be called on to solve it by working together. When world leaders develop solutions and ways of working with other countries, it is called **foreign policy**.

WRITE

In your own words, summarize the role of a world leader.

....

....

....

....

....

....

IN THE REAL WORLD

The vice president of the United States helps the president with a lot of things, but they have their own jobs too! One of the biggest roles of the vice president is to serve as president of the Senate. However, they are not allowed to vote in the Senate unless there is a tie. Then they serve as the tiebreaker!

 **READ**

World Leaders in History

Some world leaders made history for being amazing leaders, but not all! Read to learn about some of the best and worst world leaders in history.

President Abraham Lincoln of the United States of America

Abraham Lincoln was president during the Civil War. Lincoln worked to end slavery during his leadership.

President Isabel Perón of Argentina

Isabel Perón was the first woman in history to become a president. Perón was not a good leader, so the military took control of the country.

Queen Victoria of England

Queen Victoria repaired the relationship between the public and the royal family by helping the citizens have a better life.

Emperor Genghis Khan of the Mongol Empire

Genghis Khan worked to unite tribes in northeast Asia. He made himself the emperor of the Mongol Empire.

Nelson Mandela of South Africa

When South Africa first allowed all races to vote in elections in 1994, Mandela was elected the nation's first Black chief of state.

Vladimir Lenin of the Soviet Union

Vladimir Lenin was ruthless in his attempts to control Russia. He became a dictator, punishing and imprisoning anyone who disagreed with his views.

 **WRITE**   Pick two of the leaders you read about. How are they similar in their views? How are they different?

....

....

....

READ

When World Leaders Meet

When world leaders come together, each represents their home nation. This is a big responsibility. These are very formal events with a lot of attention on what happens. Sometimes these meetings are between friendly countries. Sometimes they are tense negotiations between countries that are in a disagreement. There is always an expectation that the leaders will be respectful to each other.

Even when the chiefs of state do not see eye to eye, good leaders are willing to put aside their personal feelings and differences to make the best decisions for the people they represent.

Let's look at two recent events when world leaders came together.

- **The Paris Climate Conference:** This meeting of world leaders from more than 190 nations in 2015 was a big moment in history. World leaders agreed to make changes in order to prevent irreversible climate change. The Paris Agreement is an international treaty that was created at this conference to limit global warming.
- **The G20 Summit:** The G20 Summit is an annual meeting for world leaders of the top 20 countries with the fastest growing economies. World leaders meet to discuss current economic and financial issues and how to best solve these issues.

WRITE In your own words, explain how meetings between world leaders are different from regular meetings between people.

....
....
....
....
....
....
....

REVIEW

In this lesson, you learned:

- A world leader is a chief of state, someone who leads an entire nation.
- World leaders have responsibilities in their home countries as well as globally.
- When chiefs of state interact, they have a great responsibility to act in the best interest of their people.

Think About It

What makes someone a good leader? Why would it be important for a world leader to show good leadership qualities?

Circle the correct answer.

1. What is the leader of a national government called?

   A. mayor   **C.** governor

   B. chief of state   **D.** capitano

2. Which of the following is not an important role of a world leader?

   A. being a role model

   B. providing a vision for peace

   C. sending people to prison

   D. representing their country with other leaders

3. Which of the following sentences about world leaders is true?

   A. All world leaders throughout history have been good leaders.

   B. World leaders must stay in their own countries.

   C. All world leaders serve as kings or queens.

   D. World leaders represent their home nations in world events.

4. Which statement describes the term *domestic policy*?

   A. developing solutions for challenges within one's own country

   B. developing solutions and ways of working with other countries

   C. developing solutions for challenges on other planets

   D. developing problems for other countries to solve

5. When world leaders meet, what is expected of them?

   A. They duel to solve problems.

   B. They are respectful to one another's ideas even if they do not agree.

   C. They pay one another to join forces.

   D. They agree on every aspect of foreign policy.

6. True or False   Different countries have different types of leaders.

7. True or False   World leaders never meet each other.

8. True or False   World leaders can negotiate for peace if needed.

9. In your own words, name and describe three responsibilities of a world leader.

   ....

   ....

   ....

   ....

   ....

   ....

   ....

   ....

   ....

   ....

   ....

The United Nations

By the end of this lesson, you will be able to:

- identify the role of the United Nations in the world

Lesson Review

If you need to review ways to resolve conflict in your city or country, please go to the lesson titled "Resolving Conflict."

Academic Vocabulary

Read the following vocabulary words and definitions. Look through the lesson. Can you find each vocabulary word? Underline the vocabulary word in your lesson. Write the page number of where you found each word in the blanks.

- **charter:** a set of rules (page ___)
- **dignity:** the idea that someone should be treated well and with respect (page ___)
- **global:** refers to the whole world (page ___)
- **mediate:** to work with both sides of an argument to find a solution (page ___)
- **sanction:** an action that forces a country to obey an international law (page ___)
- **United Nations:** a group of people from around the world who work together to solve big problems that can affect any global citizen (page ___)

CREATE

What does world peace mean to you? What are some basic needs that all people should have? What does a happy world look like to you? Design or decorate a peace sign symbol to demonstrate world peace. Explain your design and reasoning when you are finished.

EXPLORE

Between 1939 and 1945, many countries fought each other in a war known as World War II. Both World Wars were devastating. Millions of people died, entire countries were destroyed, and world leaders struggled to help their citizens rebuild their lives.

After the war, leaders wanted to find a way to make sure another world war never happened again. If they could find a way for people around the world to resolve their conflicts, they would be able to prevent another world war.

In April of 1945, world leaders met in San Francisco, California, to discuss how to resolve conflicts between global citizens, or citizens of the whole world. Fifty countries decided to form an international organization, like a club, that would resolve conflicts around the world.

How do you think this international organization will help prevent future world wars? Will this group be able to provide peace to all citizens?

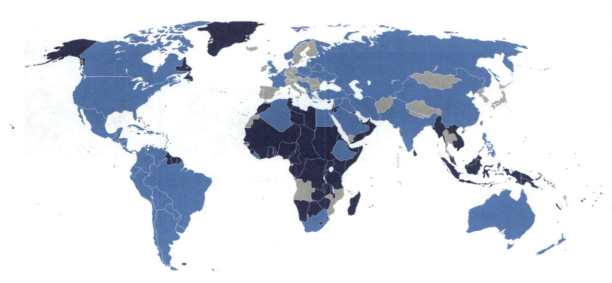

Leaders from the countries colored in light blue were original members of the international organization formed in 1945.

United Nations Member States-1945.png by Clam15 at English Wikipedia is in the public domain.

READ

What Is the United Nations?

The international organization that was formed by 50 countries at the San Francisco Conference in 1945 is called the United Nations. The **United Nations** is a group of leaders from around the world who work together to solve big problems that can affect the world.

Today, 193 countries are members of the United Nations, or UN. Each country has a representative who is part of the General Assembly. In the General Assembly, every country from the smallest to the biggest has exactly one vote and equal say in all decisions. The UN General Assembly meets every year from September to December to discuss ways to keep world peace.

The UN also has an important group called the Security Council. This smaller group is made up of 15 countries. Five of those spots are permanent members of the security council, meaning five of the most powerful countries in the world will always have a seat on the Security Council. Other countries take turns filling the other 10 spots. The Security Council identifies conflicts around the world and helps countries find peaceful solutions to their problems.

The secretary-general is the leader of the UN. This person is elected to lead and run the UN for five years. The secretary-general also mediate between countries who have conflicts. **Mediate** means to work with both sides in a argument to find a solution.

The UN logo shows a map of the world.

The UN main headquarters is located in New York.

WRITE

What is the role of the UN General Assembly? What is the role of the UN Security Council? What is the role of the secretary-general?

....

....

What Does the United Nations Do?

The main purpose of the UN is to prevent future world wars and to help countries get along. But how exactly does the UN accomplish these goals? The UN is a meeting place for countries all around the world to talk to each other and have their voices heard. The countries in the UN work together to find ways to prevent conflict between **global** citizens in the first place. If conflict still exists, the UN makes hard decisions to solve problems and enforce peace.

The UN prevents conflicts. If every global citizen has what they need to have a good life, people around the world will have less to argue about. The UN makes rules to make sure global citizens have shelter, food, medicine, safety, clean environment, education, and dignity. **Dignity** means being treated well and with respect. If the UN can help solve these major world problems, it can prevent conflict between global citizens.

The UN mediates conflict. When conflict cannot be prevented, the UN makes hard decisions to solve problems. The Security Council will vote on the best ideas to resolve conflicts in the world. The secretary-general will even act as a mediator between countries and try to find compromises.

The UN enforces peace. Sometimes countries will still have conflict that may turn violent. Every country in the UN signs a **charter**, or set of rules, that they are expected to follow. These rules are in place to help countries get along. If a country in conflict breaks one of these rules, the UN may place sanctions on them. A **sanction** is an action that forces a country to obey an international law. Many times a UN sanction stops other countries from trading goods or helping citizens in that country. In 2021, the UN had sanctions on two different countries. One sanction is on Ukraine because the leader illegally took over the country, and the second is on Iran's nuclear power program. Lastly, the UN has its own military and has the power to enforce its peacekeeping decisions. The UN's military members are known as peacekeepers.

WRITE How does the United Nations prevent conflict?

PRACTICE

Look at each real-world example in the graphic organizer. Decide if this example is the UN preventing conflict, mediating conflict, or enforcing peace. In each blank, write the words *United Nations prevents conflict, United Nations mediates conflict,* or *United Nations enforces peace.*

In Haiti, the UN is helping supply food to citizens. Haitian citizens are hungry because of bad weather for crops, high food prices, and disagreements between political leaders.	
The UN decided to send military peacekeepers to the country of Kosovo. The UN military peacekeepers are there to make sure citizens are safe.	
In the country of Malawi, a virus affected many citizens. The UN sent nurses, doctors, and medicine to help Malawi citizens.	
The UN found a compromise between the countries of Portugal and Indonesia. The two countries disagreed about a colony.	

REVIEW

In this lesson, you learned:

- The United Nations is a global organization made up of 193 countries that work together to prevent future wars and help countries get along.

- The United Nations is split into the General Assembly, Security Council, and secretary-general.

- The UN's main purposes are to prevent conflict, mediate conflict, and enforce peace.

Think About It

Out of the four main purposes for the UN, which do you believe is the most important? Discuss your thoughts with your instructor.

SHOW WHAT YOU KNOW

Use the Word Bank below to fill in the blanks to each sentence.

Word Bank: United Nations   global   dignity   charter   sanctions

1. Climate change is a _____ issue because it affects everyone in the world.

2. Every country in the United Nations votes and decides what international rules are included in the _____.

3. If a country breaks an international rule, the Security Council may decide to place _____ on that country to make them obey the rule.

4. The United Nations expects every government to treat its citizens with _____ by respecting them and providing for their well-being.

5. The 193 countries that are members of the _____ work together to prevent future wars and help countries get along.

Match each description below with the role it is describing.

6. _____ This part of the United Nations is the most powerful and made up of 15 countries.

7. _____ This part of the United Nations is made up of one representative from all 193 countries and discusses ways to keep world peace.

8. _____ This part of the United Nations is one person who is elected to run the United Nations.

A. Security Council

B. Secretary General

C. General Assembly

ONLINE CONNECTION

UNICEF is a branch of the United Nations focused solely on the well-being of children like you! Head online to research more about this incredible global organization.

Circle all the correct answers.

9. What are the United Nations' three main roles?

A. enforce peace around the world

B. organize the Olympics

C. decide who leads countries

D. prevent conflict between global citizens

E. choose sides with countries at war

F. mediate conflict between countries

Lesson 39

The Role of Media

By the end of this lesson, you will be able to:

- describe the different roles of the media in international relationships

Lesson Review

If you need to review how media can influence people and governments, please go to the lesson titled "Media and Influence."

Academic Vocabulary

Read the following vocabulary words and definitions. Look through the lesson. Can you find each vocabulary word? Underline the vocabulary word in your lesson. Write the page number where you found each word in the blanks.

- **biased:** one-sided (page ___)
- **media:** any form of communication that is shared with a large number of people (page ___)
- **propaganda:** media messages that are biased or misleading used to change people's opinions and persuade people to take a side (page ___)
- **public agenda:** a to-do list of issues that most of the public from around the world agrees are important to discuss and fix (page ___)

CREATE

Throughout history, people have made posters to try and persuade others about issues. The posters may try to get someone to take their side or support their idea.

This poster wants you to support their idea that space travel is good.

This poster wants to persuade you to vote in the next election.

Think of a problem you notice in the world around you. It may be pollution, bullies, homelessness, or your own idea. Then create your own persuasive poster to get others to support your idea.

Imagine that you notice a lot of trash on the beaches and in the ocean. It is not only gross and dirty but also is hurting wildlife. You want to solve this problem, and you need more help than just your friends— you think the whole world should work together to solve this problem! You need to get the world's attention and persuade them to be on your side. What would you do?

The media can help solve this problem. **Media** is any form of communication shared with a lot of people. For example, news outlets can share information about trash in the ocean. Billboards, posters, and social media posts can share ways to clean the beaches. A documentary could convince other countries to find better ways to deal with their trash.

Media could have an important role in solving your problem. Media has a similar role in issues all around the world.

How can the media have an impact in countries on the opposite side of the world?

....

....

....

....

....

....

IN THE REAL WORLD

In 1989, Chinese troops in Beijing forcefully removed a group of student protestors. Many were injured. Footage of the tanks in Tiananmen Square sparked global interest. Videos and images of the event were shared on almost every news channel in the world.

How do you think the media had an impact on the relationship between China and its citizens?

Type 59 tank - front right.jpg by Max Smith is in the public domain.

READ

International Relationships

International relationships are important. If countries around the world get along, then global citizens can live in peace. If countries do not get along, citizens may have to deal with conflict or war. Citizens' human rights may even become threatened. Organizations like the United Nations work to prevent and mediate conflict. They also work to enforce peace around the world. Other international organizations and citizens work to make sure all people have access to basic human needs like food, shelter, medicine, safety, a clean environment, education, and dignity.

But how do international organizations decide which issue to tackle first? How do they know what problems even exist and which issues may cause future conflict? How do citizens know what side to take in a conflict?

The media has two important roles in these international relationships. The media can bring attention to problems around the world that need to be fixed. Media can also be used to sway people's opinions and to take sides in a conflict.

REVIEW

Remember that *conflict* is a strong disagreement between people or groups that often leads to angry arguments. In this situation, conflict may be between different countries or groups of global citizens.

WRITE

What are two ways the media can impact international relationships?

....

....

....

....

....

....

Discover! SOCIAL STUDIES • GRADE 3 • LESSON 39

READ

Public Agenda

The media has an important role in helping global citizens discuss and decide which problems need to be solved first. The media helps to influence the public agenda. An agenda is like a to-do list. A citizen may have a personal agenda that includes picking up trash, voting at the next election, or participating at a city council meeting. A **public agenda** is a to-do list of issues that most of the public from around the world agrees are important to discuss and fix. The public agenda can include international issues like hunger and homelessness, rebuilding a country after an earthquake, ending a civil war, or cleaning an ocean after an oil spill.

The media gives attention to these international issues by sharing information through news outlets. Many people would never know about these important issues without hearing about them on the news. The more people who hear about problems between other countries, the more these issues become part of the public agenda. Citizens and international organizations can then step in and help solve the most important conflicts around the world.

WRITE

Describe the media's role in influencing the public agenda.

....
....
....
....
....
....

IN THE REAL WORLD

March on Washington for Jobs and Freedom, Martin Luther King, Jr. and Joachim Prinz 1963.jpg by Center for Jewish History, NYC is in the public domain.

In 1963, an estimated 250,000 people took to the streets in Washington, D.C., to protest for equal rights for Black Americans. The event was heavily televised, bringing international attention to the issue. The event's success led to the passing of the Civil Rights Act a year later. Because of the media giving this issue attention, it became part of the public agenda as a problem that was important to fix.

 **READ**

Propaganda

The media can bring attention to important world problems. It can also try and persuade people's viewpoints on international issues. **Propaganda** is media that uses biased and misleading messages to change people's opinions and persuade people to take a side. While the news has a responsibility to be factual and share information about both sides, propaganda can be **biased**, or one-sided. While some media outlets may present biased news as fact, propaganda is most often used by non-media organizations that are looking to advance their causes.

For example, a country may use posters and TV ads to convince citizens to support going to war. If the media persuades people to pick a side in a conflict, that affects relationships between countries. Often influencers are not part of the news media, but are commentators or media hosts who have a biased slant on issues.

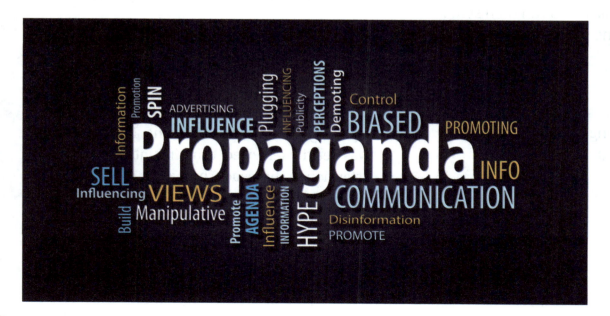

 **REVIEW**

In this lesson, you learned:

- Types of media, like news outlets and propaganda, can affect international relationships.

- Media can influence what is part of the public agenda and bring attention to world issues that need to be solved.

- Propaganda can try to convince citizens to take a side on an issue or a conflict.

Think About It

Are there any other ways the media could impact international relationships? How can the media play a role in local or national conflicts? Why is the media important to global citizens?

Match the Media Roles

Look at each example of the media influencing international relationships. Decide if each is an example of *public agenda* or *propaganda*.

2004: TSUNAMI RELIEF

In 2004, an earthquake in the Indian Ocean triggered a massive tsunami. The event was covered across print, TV, radio, and the internet. Media showed the destruction and shared people's stories. The world quickly came together and raised over $6 billion in donations.

1. ....

1942: WE CAN DO IT! POSTER

During World War II, an artist created a poster to change citizens' opinions on women working outside of their homes. Countries needed women to work in factories and make supplies for soldiers. This poster was seen by millions of people, and many women were convinced to proudly work in factories during the war.

2. ....

SHOW WHAT YOU KNOW

Use the word bank below to fill in the blanks in each sentence:

Word Bank: propaganda media biased public agenda

1. The documentary about illegal fishing in the seas around China was _____ because it only showed one side of the issue.

2. The news shared information about a protest in Europe. All of this attention help to make the issue important and part of the _____.

3. News, movies, internet, magazines, books, radio, and advertisements are all forms of _____ because they share information with a large group of people.

4. A radio station in Australia used _____ to try and convince people to vote in favor of a new law.

Circle the correct answers.

5. What are the two main roles of the media in international relations? Select all that apply.

   A. to entertain global citizens

   B. to change people's opinions and to take sides in a conflict

   C. to bring attention to problems around the world that need to be fixed

   D. to show how one country is better than another

PLAY

Imagine you are a TV news reporter. Create a skit where you are reporting on news from around the world. Include stories about conflicts and issues that are happening in other countries. You can even ask an adult to help you come up with ideas!

6. True or False   The media can help influence the public agenda.

7. True or False   Some media, like propaganda, can be biased.

8. True or False   The public agenda makes citizens and organizations ignore problems in the world.

9. True or False   No one in the world ever takes sides in conflicts.

Lesson 40

How Countries Work Together

By the end of this lesson, you will be able to:

- identify ways countries work together or help each other

Lesson Review

If you need to review the United Nations, please go to the lesson titled "The United Nations."

Academic Vocabulary

Read the following vocabulary words and definitions. Look through the lesson. Can you find each vocabulary word? Underline the vocabulary word in your lesson. Write the page number of where you found each word in the blanks.

- **globalization:** the way countries and people of the world interact (page ____)
- **trade:** the transfer or exchange of goods and services (page ____)
- **United Nations:** a group of people from all around the world who work together to solve big problems that can affect any global citizen (page ____)

PLAY.

What does working together mean to you? When was the last time your family worked together? Did it make the task easier?

Gather some blocks and use them to build a tower with your family. First, build the tower with no communication. Do not talk or gesture to each other. How do you think it will go? Next try with verbal communication. For example, you can say "I need the red block," or you can come up with a building strategy with your family. Which way was the most difficult? Which way was easiest?

EXPLRE

To live in the world, countries need to work together because Earth is everyone's home. You have already learned about the **United Nations**, which is made up of leaders from 193 different countries. They are in charge of managing international conflict. That means the issues involve more than one country. Together, the United Nations strives toward world peace. Its goal is to maintain peace and security for all the world's citizens. Nations work together outside of the United Nations as well. Countries **trade**, lend support in crisis, and try to solve global issues such as the COVID-19 outbreak.

Think about how your family works together. Do you ever trade toys with your sibling? When someone is sick, do you help care for them? Families work together to solve problems, create memories, and keep peace.

Pretend your family wants to go on a vacation. Your family might vote to decide where to go. Then you could figure out how to save money for the trip. Think about this. How would a family work together?

....
....
....
....
....
....
....
....
....
....
....
....

IN THE REAL WORLD

Countries must work together in trade, during a natural disaster, or for fun. Countries around the world come together for the Olympics. The Olympic Games are a beautiful example of countries putting aside their differences in order to celebrate the world's best athletes.

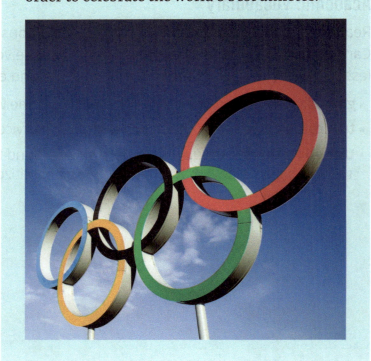

READ

Globalization

Globalization describes the way countries and people of the world interact. Globalization has many sides and can be economic, political, or cultural.

Economic globalization is how countries come together as one big economy, making international trade easier. The internet and other communication technologies make it easier for people to buy and sell products from around the world. This is an example of globalization.

Political globalization is the development and influence of international organizations. The United Nations is an example of this because most countries are members. This international organization can make countries follow rules and apply economic action to countries who do not. This means the countries in the United Nations will punish them by not talking to or trading with them so that they do not benefit from globalization.

Cultural globalization is how different cultures are combined with each other. For example, many people around the world write with the Latin alphabet, wear T-shirts and jeans, and watch Hollywood movies and other media.

Three Types of Globalization

Type of Globalization	Its Role
Economic	international trade
Political	international agencies like the United Nations
Cultural	how we are similar around the world

WRITE

What are the three types of globalization?

....

....

....

....

....

Examples of Countries Working Together

The Universal Declaration of Human Rights states fundamental rights and freedoms for all. The General Assembly of the United Nations adopted it in 1948. It declares that human rights are universal—to be enjoyed by all people, no matter who they are or where they live. The Universal Declaration includes civil and political rights, like the right to life, liberty, free speech, and privacy. This is an example of political globalization.

In December 2004, Southeast Asia was hit by a 9.0 earthquake and a tsunami that killed more than 280,000 people across 14 nations. The international community pledged billions of dollars to assist in recovery. This is an example of economic globalization.

The World Health Organization (WHO) is leading and coordinating the global effort to prevent, detect, and respond to the COVID-19 pandemic that began in 2020. The WHO is an example of political globalization. They helped develop rapid testing for COVID-19 and aided vaccine development. Wearing masks over the nose and mouth to prevent illness has become fashionable. This is an example of cultural globalization.

The European Union (EU) sent 50 tons of protective equipment to China where the coronavirus outbreak began. When the pandemic later hit Europe, China sent supplies and equipment to the EU. This is an example of countries working together and supporting each other.

Describe one example of countries working together in your own words.

Universal Declaration of Human Rights

Let's look at the first three articles defining universal human rights.

Article 1

"All human beings are born free and equal in dignity and rights. They are endowed with reason and conscience and should act toward one another in a spirit of brotherhood."

Article 2

"Everyone is entitled to all the rights and freedoms set forth in this Declaration, without distinction of any kind, such as race, color, sex, language, religion, political or other opinion, national or social origin, property, birth or other status...."

Article 3

"Everyone has the right to life, liberty, and security of person."

READ

How Countries Work Together in Today's World

As our world develops, connections between countries also grow. With advances in travel, we are able to go more places, making trade easier. Technological growth allows us to translate languages and meet with people virtually, which makes it easier for different countries to work together.

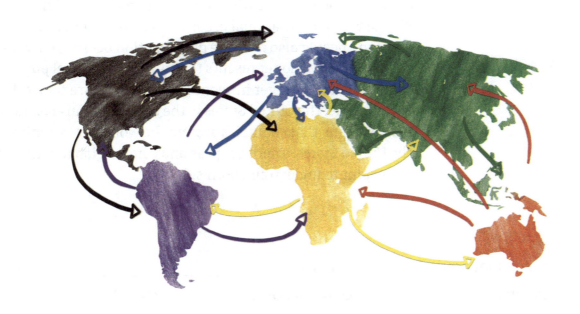

REVIEW

In this lesson, you learned:

- The three types of globalization, or the way countries and people of the world interact, are economic, political, and cultural.

Think About It
Out of the three types of globalization, which do you think is the most important? Discuss with your instructor.

PRACTICE

Match each international action to its type of globalization.

1. economic

A. the creation of the World Health Organization (WHO)

2. political

B. smiling at people

3. cultural

C. trade between two countries

SHOW WHAT YOU KNOW

Circle the correct answer.

1. What type of globalization is the United Nations?

   A. political

   B. economic

   C. cultural

   D. none of the above

2. Countries donating money to help Southeast Asia after the 2004 tsunami is what type of globalization?

   A. political

   B. economic

   C. cultural

   D. none of the above

TAKE A CLOSER LOOK

Globalization has done a lot of good, but many countries dislike when international organizations tell them what to do. Many people also criticize globalization because citizens can not decide who represents them.. Also, some feel powerful countries have a bigger influence on world culture than others. For example, the United States is the biggest cultural exporter, which means that countries around the world are becoming like the United States. There are pros and cons to globalization. It is important to understand both sides.

Fill in the blanks with the correct words.

3. People smiling at each other and using the Latin alphabet around the world are examples of _____ globalization.

4. An example of _____ globalization is the creation of the Universal Declaration of Human Rights.

Answer the following question in complete sentences.

5. In your own words, describe an example of political globalization. Explain why it is political globalization.

....

....

....

....

....

Lesson 41
Trade

By the end of this lesson, you will be able to:

- define the term *trade*
- explain why trading between countries is important

Lesson Review

If you need to review globalization, please go to the lesson titled "How Countries Work Together."

Academic Vocabulary

Read the following vocabulary words and definitions. Look through the lesson. Can you find each vocabulary word? Underline the vocabulary word in your lesson. Write the page number where you found each word in the blanks.

- **domestic trade:** trade within the country (page ___)
- **export:** a product or service produced in one country but sold to another country (page ___)
- **globalization:** the way countries and people around the world interact (page ___)
- **import:** to bring goods in from another country (page ___)
- **international trade:** trade with another country (page ___)
- **trade:** the transfer or exchange of goods and services (page ___)

PLAY.

When playing some board games, you need to trade something to advance in the game. Find a board game, such as Catan or Monopoly, that involves trade. Trade is offering something in exchange for something you would like. For example, in Monopoly you might trade a property for a different one you need. Does trading help you in the game? If so, how? If you do not have a game that requires trading, you can play an online version.

Trade, or the transfer or exchange of goods and services, has developed with civilization. Take a look at ancient Mesopotamia (a region of western Asia), Iraq, and parts of Turkey, Iran, Syria, and Kuwait. In Mesopotamia trade developed as the civilization grew. With more people living in cities, not everyone spent their days providing food for their families. They started to trade amongst themselves to provide for their families. This also meant people from the countryside were bringing goods into the city. Thanks to the development of the wheel and sail, transportation of goods became easier for the Mesopotamians. This allowed heavy goods to be put into rolling carts, which were often pushed by oxen. Since wheels were unable to travel long distances over varying terrain, Mesopotamians used donkeys to carry their goods. Donkeys are surprisingly strong and can hold up to 150 pounds on their backs. Today we do not need donkeys or oxen to transport our goods. Now we have trains, trucks, airplanes, and cargo ships. These modes of transportation carry goods around the world.

How did the people of Mesopotamia transport their goods?

....

....

....

The region that was once Mesopotamia

TAKE A CLOSER LOOK

Trading in Mesopotamia

What did the people of Mesopotamia trade? The fertile land and development of agriculture made this area rich with resources. As a result, they traded an assortment of fruits and vegetables, nuts, dairy, fish, and meat. Additionally, Mesopotamia used clay and mud to build their cities. They also used these to make and trade bowls and pots. The area did not have metal ores or timber, which meant they needed to rely on trade for those resources. This is why trade between countries and regions is important—so people can have access to things they otherwise would not.

READ

What Is Trade?

Trade is the transfer or exchange of goods and services. We go to the grocery store and trade money for our grocery items. We need money to buy necessities, so people get jobs and trade their services for money. A doctor trades their medical aid to patients in exchange for money. A baker trades their service of baking a cake for financial gain. Trade also happens on a grander scale. For instance, Alaska cannot grow avocados. In order to get avocados, they will need to trade with another state such as California.

International and Domestic Trade

Trade can be domestic or international. **Domestic trade** is trade within a country. For example, if the state of Washington trades apples with the state of New Mexico, that is domestic trade because both states are located in the United States. **International trade** is trade with another country. For example, if Mexico trades corn, soybeans, dairy, pork, and beef products to Germany in exchange for cars, that is international trade.

Import and Export

An **import** is a good or service being received from another country. Produce received into the United States from Mexico is an import. Imports are the goods coming into a country, and **exports** are the goods going out of a country. An export of the United States may be vehicles to other countries such as Canada.

A cargo ship with imports and exports

WRITE

What is an example of international trade?

....

....

....

 **READ**

Why Is Trade Between Countries Important?

International trade is important because it increases standard of living, access to resources, and economic growth. International trade is an example of economic **globalization**, or how countries come together as one big global economy. Through trading internationally, we are able to share resources to better the entire world.

Some countries have an abundance of raw materials such as oil, metal, electricity, and produce. Through international trade, other countries can benefit from these materials. For example, Iceland imports bauxite, which is needed to produce aluminum, and uses it to make aluminum, which it then exports. This is an example of important trade between countries because if Iceland could not import bauxite, they could not export aluminum.

With the expansion of international trade, our choices also increase. For example, instead of just two types of hot sauce made from local peppers, we have shelves of hot sauce choices with a variety of spices and flavors. Having a variety of selections available allows more people to enjoy the product and increases the standard of living.

International trade helps economic growth worldwide because it increases the number of jobs and availability of resources, which reduces poverty. Countries participating in international trade tend to grow and develop faster than other countries. Countries trading with each other support everyone's economic growth.

 **TAKE A CLOSER LOOK**

Advantages of International Trade for the Consumer

A consumer is someone who purchases a good or service to use. We are consumers when we buy electronics, groceries, hire a cleaning service, or travel. International trade has numerous benefits to us including employment opportunities, choices, and lower costs. Trade comes with job growth because when demand rises, so does the need for workers. With trade, consumers get more choices. Having more products available through imports and exports helps to lower the cost of products.

WRITE   What is one benefit of international trade?

....
....
....
....
....
....
....
....

PRACTICE

Match the correct trade factor to its benefit.

FACTOR

1. ____ products from various countries

2. ____ rise in demand for a product/resource

3. ____ ability to trade an abundant resource

4. ____ importing essential resources

BENEFIT

A. able to have a financial gain from resources

B. more choices for the consumer

C. increased availability to resources

D. growth in job opportunities

REVIEW

In this lesson, you learned:

- Trade is the transfer or exchange of goods and services.

- International trade is trade among different countries.

- International trade is important for global growth and development.

Think About It

What would you not be able to eat or use if not for international trade? Consider what resources your area has and what it does not have.

SHOW WHAT YOU KNOW

Circle the correct answer for each question.

1. What is one example of international trade?

   A. trading a friend an apple for a banana

   B. Idaho exporting potatoes

   C. United States importing maple syrup from Canada

   D. taking a vacation from Nebraska to California

2. What is the difference between an import and an export?

   A. Imports are goods brought into the country, and exports are goods going out of the country.

   B. Exports are goods brought into the country, and imports are goods going out of the country.

   C. Imports are resources, and exports are services.

   D. Exports are resources, and imports are services.

Fill in the blanks with the correct word.

3. When the United States exports vehicles to another country, it is an example of _____ trade.

4. Maple syrup is an _____ to the United States from Canada.

5. Define *trade*.

   ....
   ....
   ....
   ....

ONLINE CONNECTION

Research your country's imports and exports. Before heading to the computer, make a list of items you think your country exports. How many did you get correct? Which one surprised you? What was your country's biggest export? What was your country's biggest import? Discuss your findings with your instructor.

Lesson 42

Conflicts Among Countries

By the end of this lesson, you will be able to:

- identify types of conflicts that can occur in the world

Lesson Review

If you need to review globalization, please go to the lesson titled "How Countries Work Together."

Academic Vocabulary

Read the following vocabulary words and definitions. Look through the lesson. Can you find each vocabulary word? Underline the vocabulary word in your lesson. Write the page number of where you found each word in the blanks.

- **economic sanctions:** trade barriers (page ___)
- **export:** a product or service produced in one country but sold to another country (page ___)
- **import:** to bring a good in from another country (page ___)
- **international conflict:** when two different countries strongly disagree (page ___)
- **territorial disputes:** a disagreement over the possession or control of land or water (page ___)

World War 1

The year was 1939 when Germany invaded Poland. Great Britain and France responded by declaring war on Germany, thus starting World War II. This war was the result of an international conflict of ideas, land disputes, and economic stress worldwide. This war involved almost every part of the world. The two sides that fought the war were called the Axis powers (Germany, Italy, and Japan) and the Allies (United States, the Soviet Union, the United Kingdom, and France).

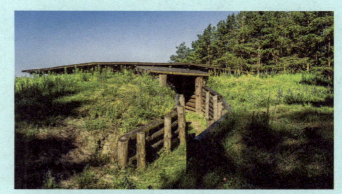

An entrance to an old wooden bunker from World War I.

Have you ever disagreed with someone? How do you resolve disagreements? Perhaps you and a friend disagree on a movie. You might discuss your options and compromise so both of you are happy. Maybe the conflict is more complicated, such as your friend hanging out with people who leave you out. How can you resolve this? Do you tell your friend to stop hanging out with them? Do you talk to the group? It is a lot harder when more people are involved.

Countries have conflicts too, and they can be difficult to sort out. In 1754 there was a dispute over land in North America between the French and the English. Both countries wanted control of the Ohio River. This led to the Seven Years' War, which ended when the Treaty of Paris was signed in 1763. Sometimes conflicts can be ended peacefully by negotiating and compromising. An example of this was when the presidents of the Republic of Kazakhstan and Uzbekistan peacefully signed a compromise over a border dispute.

What is a conflict you have had in your life? How did you resolve it?

....
....
....
....
....
....
....
....
....
....
....
....
....
....

A map of the Republic of Kazakhstan and Uzbekistan.

READ

International Conflicts

An **international conflict** is when two different countries strongly disagree. This can cause them to stop trading with each other or even lead to war. Typically conflicts are born from opposing interests. For instance, the Cold War, between the United States and the Soviet Union, came from opposing interests over political ideals and control. The Soviets wanted to spread the political idea of communism, a political idea advocating for a classless system where all property is communal property. The United States feared the communists coming to power. This resulted in the Cold War, which did not result in military combat. Instead it became a competition between the United States and the Soviet Union to have alliances with newly independent nations after the Second World War. The Cold War is an example of a conflict of ideas. Other conflicts can come from economic disputes and disputes over land and water. These conflicts can result in a ban on trade between countries, war, or negotiating a settlement to their differences.

Effects of International Conflicts

There are many effects when countries have disputes. War is often a consequence of international conflict. Another effect is resource use. For example, if a country is at war, the resources will go toward war efforts before going to the general public. When conflicts turn violent, it can result in forced migration, where people flee their homes to other countries as refugees in order to stay safe. These conflicts can also result in lives lost and property destroyed. Additionally, if the cost to import an item rises, it can cause financial hardship and lack of access to resources. Leaders must navigate these costs and decide the best plan to keep their country safe and thriving.

WRITE

What is an international conflict?

....

....

....

TAKE A CLOSER LOOK

The Cold War began after the Second World War in 1945. From 1945–1991, there was tension between the democracies of the Western world and the communist countries of Eastern Europe. The countries never officially declared war on each other, but they did fight in proxy wars. Proxy wars are fought between other countries, but with each side getting support from different powerful countries, such as the United States and the Soviet Union. They also competed with technology. This was seen in the Space Race, where both countries tried to be the first to land on the moon.

 **READ**

Three Themes of Conflicts

There are three themes of international conflict: territorial disputes, conflicts of ideas, and economic conflicts. These disputes can affect the people living in those countries. They can lead to war, a decrease in economic growth, migration, and a decrease in essential goods due to low resources.

Territorial disputes are when two countries disagree over control of land or water. They are often related to the possession of natural resources or to culture, religion, or ethnic nationalism. For example, Israel and Palestine have a dispute over a piece of land called the West Bank. It includes sites that hold cultural, historical, and religious significance for both countries, thus causing a land dispute.

Conflicts of ideas are having opposing interests, as seen in the Cold War between the United States and the Soviet Union. This can be a result of differing values, how to handle a task, or the relations between two nations.

Economic conflicts are disputes over resources. When the world economy is not growing, there is a higher chance for conflict, especially over essential resources. Another example of an international economic conflict is placing **economic sanctions**, which means another country places a barrier on trade. A country may raise the cost to **export** a product, which could cause other countries to struggle to **import** and access that product.

 **IN THE REAL WORLD**

World War II and the Need for Nylon

During times of conflict, people in those countries have to make sacrifices. One item the United States needed for military use was nylon. It was needed for parachutes, glider tow ropes, aircraft fuel tanks, shoelaces, mosquito netting, and hammocks. Women of the time wore nylon stockings. Due to the high demand for nylon, the women had to give up their stockings. Instead they used liquid silk stockings, also called paint!

WRITE   What are the three types of international conflicts?

....

....

....

....

PRACTICE

Identify the type of conflict for each statement.

A. Territorial Disputes

B. Conflicts of Ideas

C. Economic Conflicts

1. _____ not trading with a country

2. _____ disagreeing on political ideas

3. _____ disagreeing about religion

4. _____ disagreeing on who controls an island

5. _____ raising the cost to export a product to another country

6. _____ disputing a border

7. _____ disagreeing on who has control over a river

REVIEW

In this lesson, you learned:

- Three themes of international conflicts are territorial conflicts, conflicts of ideas, and economic conflicts.

- International conflicts can have major impacts on the world.

Think About It

Do you think these conflicts result in difficult relationships between countries after the conflict has been resolved? What might be done to resolve that type of conflict?

SHOW WHAT YOU KNOW

Match each vocabulary word to the correct definition.

1. _____ territorial disputes

2. _____ international conflict

3. _____ economic sanctions

4. _____ import

5. _____ export

A. when two different countries strongly disagree

B. a product or service produced in one country but sold to another country

C. a disagreement over the possession or control of land or water

D. to bring a good in from another country

E. trade barriers

Circle the correct answer.

6. What is NOT an effect from an international conflict?

A. war

B. decrease of resources

C. people leaving their countries to find safety

D. economic growth

7. In your own words, describe one type of international conflict: territorial, ideas, or economic.

....

....

....

....

ONLINE CONNECTION

Research a past conflict between countries. Some examples are the Cold War, the American Revolution, the Vietnam War, or the World Wars. Answer these questions:

- What countries were involved in the conflict?
- How did the conflict begin?
- How was the conflict resolved?

Conflict Resolution

By the end of this lesson, you will be able to:

- explain compromise as a conflict resolution strategy
- describe examples of international conflicts that were resolved through compromise
- describe examples of international conflict where war is needed

Lesson Review

If you need to review types of conflicts, please go to the lesson titled "Conflicts Among Countries."

Academic Vocabulary

Read the following vocabulary words and definitions. Look through the lesson. Can you find each vocabulary word? Underline the vocabulary word in your lesson. Write the page number of where you found each word in the blanks.

- **conflict resolution:** a peaceful way to agree to end a disagreement (page ____)
- **consensus:** countries either agree or disagree when making a decision (page ____)
- **NATO:** North Atlantic Treaty Organization (page ____)
- **peace treaty:** an agreement between two or more countries to end a war (page ____)
- **United Nations:** a group of people from around the world who work together to solve big problems that can affect any global citizen (page ____)

IN THE REAL WORLD

In June 1919, at the Palace of Versailles in Paris, France, the Treaty of Versailles was signed by Germany and the Allied countries. The Treaty of Versailles is a peace treaty, an agreement between two or more countries to end a war. This was one of the most important treaties in history as it ended World War I and created peace among all countries. It recognized that Germany was responsible for starting the war between the Axis powers and the Allies. The opposing countries, also known as the Central Powers, were Germany, Austria-Hungary, and Turkey.

The Palace of Versailles

EXPLORE

Think back to a time where you had a disagreement with someone. Maybe it was a brother or a sister or a friend. What were the things you said to the other person to resolve the conflict or disagreement? How did you feel after the disagreement was resolved? Normally, when there is a compromise, or **conflict resolution**, each person agrees to things that benefit both people.

Countries have compromised through conflict resolution as well. When the Treaty of Versailles, a **peace treaty**, was signed in Paris in 1919, Germany admitted responsibility for the war. As a result, the conflict resolution, identified in the treaty, was that their military had to be reduced, they lost territory, and they had to pay large amounts of money to civilians for the damage the country inflicted during the war. Throughout history, some international conflicts were resolved where one or more countries benefited more than the others. Unfortunately, this led to more problems and was one of the reasons World War II began.

A trench from World War I

TAKE A CLOSER LOOK

Mahatma Gandhi was an activist from India who championed conflict resolution through peaceful means. He lived from 1869–1948.

Gandhi was best known for the following things:

- using nonviolent methods of conflict resolution to gain India's independence from British rule
- inspiring civil rights and freedom movements around the world using his peaceful conflict resolution strategies
- inspiring Martin Luther King Jr. during the civil rights movement in the United States

READ

Compromise and Conflict Resolution

Throughout history, countries have compromised to resolve conflicts instead of entering into war. For example, the Cold War was an ongoing political rivalry between the United States, the Soviet Union, and their allies that developed after World War II. The Cold War lasted until 1991. During this time, the United States and the Soviet Union did not declare war. Instead, threats of war occured to scare one another.

NATO

The United States and its European allies formed **NATO**, or the North Atlantic Treaty Organization, to resist the Soviet Union's presence in Europe in 1949. NATO currently has 30 countries within its membership including the United States. NATO's purpose is to provide freedom and security to its members through military means and ongoing discussion.

A NATO Monument in Brussels

WRITE

Why do you think it is important that NATO has ongoing discussions with other countries? How might these discussions affect other countries' relationships with one another?

The Flag of NATO

READ

NATO's Purpose

NATO's job is to protect the freedom and security of its member countries. These countries engage in conversation to make decisions about security and how to maintain peace within nations. All decisions are made by **consensus**, where all member countries either agree or disagree.

NATO accomplishes its purpose through political discussion, military means, and collective defense. NATO promotes democracy where citizens of nations hold the power. To maintain democracy within countries, it uses conflict resolution through ongoing discussions with nations that disagree with one another. NATO also protects other countries through military means. Sometimes conflict among nations cannot be resolved through peaceful dialogue and compromise. If these efforts fail, it uses military power to engage in war with those who fail to compromise.

NATO believes that an attack on one of its member countries is an attack on all of its countries. This is called collective defense. Collective defense has been invoked once, when the September 11th attacks occurred in the United States. This is an example of countries having to go to war to obtain peace. The United States and other countries within NATO engaged in war with Afghanistan due to the attacks.

WRITE

Think about NATO's purpose. Why do you think the 30 countries who belong chose to join?

....

....

....

....

....

....

....

....

....

READ

War

Sometimes resolution cannot be obtained through peaceful compromise, like when both countries cannot come to an agreement without using war. One example of when this occurred was when the war on terror began, also known as the War in Afghanistan.

The September 11th attacks, also known as 9/11, prompted the War in Afghanistan to begin. President George W. Bush declared war on Afghanistan and demanded that the Taliban, the group responsible for the 9/11 events, turn over its leader, Osama bin Laden, to the US government.

The Taliban refused to do so. As a result, Operation Enduring Freedom, a global war effort to eliminate the Taliban, was launched. Great Britain was a major ally to the United States in this effort. By December 2001, the United States and its allies were able to drive the Taliban out of power. However, many of its members were not captured and escaped to Pakistan.

The **United Nations**, a group of people from around the world who work together to solve big problems that can affect any global citizen, adopted the Security Council Resolution 1368 as a result of the 9/11 attacks. It condemned the attacks on the United States and relayed it was determined to combat threats to international peace and security caused by acts of terrorism.

The United Nations Building in Geneva

The Flag of the United Nations

WRITE

Why do you think declaring war was necessary in order for the United States to defeat the Taliban and restore peace?

....

....

....

....

PRACTICE

1. What were two things Mahatma Gandhi did?

....

....

....

....

2. Why did the War in Afghanistan begin?

....

....

....

....

3. What happened as a result of Operation Enduring Freedom?

....

....

....

....

....

4. Name three things that NATO does. Why are these three things important for solving conflicts?

....

....

....

....

....

REVIEW

In this lesson, you learned:

- Conflict resolution can occur through peaceful ways to obtain compromise.
- Conflict resolution can also occur when two or more countries go to war to arrive at a solution.
- A peace treaty is an agreement to end conflict between two or more countries.

Think About It
What are some ways that you might use peaceful compromise in your own life?

Circle the correct answer.

1. What did the Treaty of Versailles do?

   A. ended the War in Afghanistan

   B. ended World War I

   C. ended Operation Freedom

   D. was created by Mahatma Gandhi

2. What does NATO do?

   A. makes sure other countries have the safety and security to protect those who live there

   B. created peace during World War I

   C. makes decisions about how countries should run

   D. seeks to end world hunger

ONLINE CONNECTION

With an adult's help, use a search engine to research civil disobedience to learn about how more world leaders used it to resolve conflict. Identify two leaders who used civil disobedience to arrive at peace. Discuss with your instructor how they used it to compromise.

Fill in the blanks with the correct words.

3. Mahatma Gandhi used _____ as a peaceful strategy to resolve conflict.

4. _____ is a world organization dedicated to promoting peace.

Answer the following question in complete sentences.

5. Do you think it is better for leaders to engage in war or discussions first to arrive at a compromise? Explain your answer.

....

....

....

....

Chapter 9 Review

By the end of this lesson, you will:

- review the information from the lessons in Chapter 9, "International Relationships."

Lesson Review

Throughout the chapter, we have learned the following big ideas:

- Countries work together in different ways to solve all kinds of issues. (Lesson 40)
- Trade is important for countries and helps grow the world's economy. (Lesson 41)
- World conflict can be caused by territorial disputes, conflicts of ideas, or economic conflicts. (Lesson 42)
- Countries solve problems through conflict resolution, which often involves compromise. (Lesson 43)

Go back and review the lessons as needed while you complete the activities.

ONLINE CONNECTION

There are many great resources online to show you the importance of world trade and why it occurs. Look online and see if you can find real world examples of how countries have traded with one another and what kinds of things are traded. Take care to note the amount of money that is exchanged for goods.

REVIEW

What Is Globalization?

Let's review what globalization is and the types of globalization that exist. Globalization describes the way countries and people of the world interact and integrate. Globalization can be divided into three types. Economic globalization is how countries come together as one big global economy, making international trade easier. Political globalization is the development and growing influence of international organizations. Cultural globalization is how culture is becoming more similar.

What Is Trade?

Trade is the transfer or exchange of goods and services. We need food. We go to the grocery store and trade money for our grocery items. Trade is important because we need money to buy necessities, so people get a job trading their services for money. What are international and domestic trade, and how are they different? The trade among states is domestic trade. Trade to another country is international trade.

Import and Export

An import is a good or service being received. The United States selling electronics to Mexico is an export. Imports are the goods coming into a country, and exports are the goods going out of a country.

WRITE

What are some examples of how countries import and export goods? Can you think of two?

....

....

....

....

....

REVIEW

International Conflict

We have also learned about international conflicts. When two different countries strongly disagree, it can lead to a trade ban or even war between the countries.

Can you remember what the three themes of international conflict are?

- Territorial disputes: These disputes over who controls an area of land or water can affect the people living in those countries. It can lead to war, economic decrease in growth, migration, and decrease in essential goods due to low resources.

- Conflicts of ideas: Conflicts of ideas are opposing interests, as seen in the Cold War between the United States and the Soviet Union. This can be a result of differing values, different ideas of how to handle a task, or the relationship between two nations.

- Economic conflicts: Economic conflicts are disputes over resources. Economic growth helps lower the level of conflict. Therefore, when the world economy is not growing, there is a higher chance for conflict, especially over essential resources.

Once you learned what the three themes of international conflict were, we explored the definition of conflict resolution and how countries solve it through compromise. However, some conflicts cannot always be resolved peacefully through compromise. NATO and the United Nations help countries resolve conflicts peacefully. One example of a conflict that led to war was the War in Afghanistan after the 9/11 attacks occurred. A conflict resolution example is when countries signed the Treaty of Versailles, which ended World War I in 1919.

Helpful Hints

Here are some helpful tips to think about the big ideas from this chapter:

- The three types of globalization are economic, political, and cultural.

- Conflict sometimes is resolved peacefully, but sometimes it results in war.

- An import is a good entering a country (Think of import as "in.")

- An export is a good that a country sells to another country. (Think of an export as "exiting.")

PRACTICE

Vocabulary Memory Game

1. Using the vocabulary words below, write each term on one side of an index card. On a second index card, write only the definition.

2. Shuffle the index cards and line them up face down like you would if you were playing the game Memory.

3. Taking turns, flip one of the cards over and locate its respective definition by flipping another card over. The person with the most matches wins!

- **conflict resolution:** a peaceful way to agree to end a disagreement
- **consensus:** countries coming to a general agreement when making a decision
- **domestic trade:** trade within the country
- **export:** a product or service produced in one country but sold to another country
- **globalization:** the way countries and people of the world interact
- **import:** to bring a good in from another country
- **international conflict:** when two different countries strongly disagree
- **international trade:** trade with another country
- **NATO:** North Atlantic Treaty Organization
- **peace treaty:** an agreement between two or more countries to end a war
- **territorial disputes:** when two countries disagree over control of an area of land or water
- **trade:** the transfer or exchange of goods and services
- **United Nations:** a global organization dedicated to world peace

Vocabulary Tips
One way to remember your vocabulary words and their definitions is to draw the meaning of what each vocabulary word represents. For example, for the word *consensus*, you could draw two people shaking hands to represent they have come to an agreement.

PRACTICE

Graphic Organizer

In this activity, you will create a graphic organizer to help you remember the three types of globalization (political, economic, and cultural). Here are the steps:

1. In the circles below, write "Types of Globalization" in the center circle.

2. Write each type of globalization in one of the three other circles.

3. Write the definitions and characteristics that represent each term.

4. Refer back to this graphic organizer to help you remember some of the big ideas from the chapter!

Interesting Facts About NATO:

- Countries have to pay to be a part of NATO. It costs about $3,000,000 per year to run NATO.

- NATO has other partners, like the United Nations and the European Union, who are not members.

- NATO defends its members against land, sea, air, and cyber attacks.

- Since 2014, NATO has deployed NATO forces to Estonia, Latvia, Lithuania, and Poland to prevent conflict.

- In 1949, when NATO was established, there were only 12 member countries.

- There are two official languages of NATO, English and French.

NATO Monument in Brussels

PRACTICE

International Conflict

1. Create a graphic organizer like the one below to remember the three types of international conflict.

2. List each type of international conflict in the boxes in the top row.

3. List the various traits below each box for each type of conflict.

Territorial Disputes	Conflicts of Ideas	Economic Conflicts

Chapter 10
World History

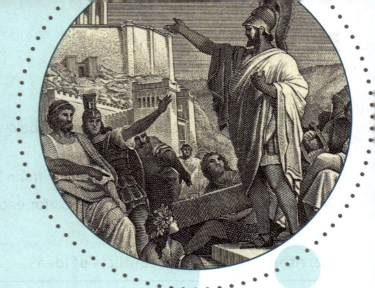

Hi! Julia, the grasshopper here!

Last time, we got bad news. The United States and Mexico had stopped trading wheat for corn.

We took an airplane to New York because it is too far to hop! I knew we had important work to do. My cousins and I knew that trading between countries was important. It was our job to tell the world's leaders about it.

Do you want to hear what happened at the United Nations? Let's hop to it!

I read all about the United Nations before going there. Fun fact: It was formed in 1945 to help countries work together. It was formed the year after World War II ended.

Our plane landed in New York. We took a taxi to the United Nations building surrounded by all the flags of the world.

I walked in and met my cousins. We were so happy to see each other. We jumped up and down. After saying hello, we walked into the main hall.

The main hall has hundreds of seats—one desk for every country in the world.

There is a big stage in the middle. That is where we will talk! I was nervous. But I knew that good things come to those who hustle.

Still, can a bunch of grasshoppers convince leaders and presidents to do the right thing? Only one way to find out!

What Will I Learn?

This chapter looks at world history and how it is understood. It looks at different perspectives and approaches to the past and how cooperation can be encouraged in the future.

Lessons at a Glance

Lesson 45

Past, Present, Future

By the end of this lesson, you will be able to:

- identify the difference between past, present, and future using timelines and other geographic representations

Lesson Review

If you need to review physical features, please go to the lesson titled "Discovering Physical Features."

Academic Vocabulary

Read the following vocabulary words and definitions. Look through the lesson. Can you find each vocabulary word? Underline the vocabulary word in your lesson. Write the page number of where you found each word in the blanks.

- **chronological:** the order of events (page ____)
- **future:** the time that has not happened yet (page ____)
- **past:** any time that has already happened (page ____)
- **present:** the time happening right now (page ____)
- **primary source:** accounts from people who witnessed the events (page ____)
- **secondary source:** written after the event has taken place (page ____)
- **timeline:** a display of events that have happened chronologically (page ____)

IN THE REAL WORLD

If it is getting dark and you want to keep reading a book, what could you use to see? Do you think what you use today is different from what people used long ago? You might use a lamp or a flashlight. Before light bulbs were invented, people used candlelight.

Things change over the years. Indoor plumbing has not always existed. Before indoor plumbing, people would fill buckets with water to fill the bathtub. Now, we use the faucet to fill the bathtub, which is much easier. Many other items have changed over time. Take a look at how the phone has changed through time.

Another example of how things have changed is how we warm our homes. In the past, there was nothing like heaters controlled by thermostats. People would have to build a fire to warm the house. Now people can control the heat to the exact temperature they want.

How has life changed from when your instructor, family member, grandparent, or grown-up was a kid? Fill out the Venn diagram below. Compare what life today is like to when they were a child. Also, find what is similar between being a kid today and in the past.

_____   _____

BOTH

READ

Past, Present, and Future

The past means anything that has already happened. The past can be yesterday or many years ago. When we read from history books, they are talking about events in the past. We learn about the past through **primary sources**, which are accounts from people who witnessed the events. Another way we know about the past is through **secondary sources** written after the event has taken place.

The **present** is what is occurring now. We are all living in the present right now. We can learn about the present by watching and reading the news. Many ways we know what is happening right now are through primary sources.

The **future** is what is going to happen. We do not know the future, but we can predict what might happen by understanding the past. So we can make educated guesses, but no one really knows what will happen.

A **timeline** is a display of events that have happened chronologically. **Chronological** means the order of events: first, second, and third. Look at this timeline about music. We can see the record player and CD are in the past, and digital music is the present.

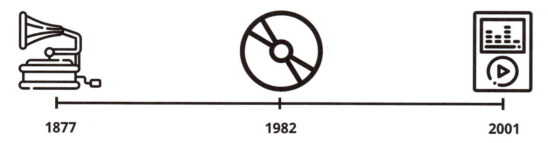

| 1877 | 1982 | 2001 |

Timelines can tell about events in the past and present. Sometimes people put future predictions on timelines, but that is just a guess. It does not mean it will actually happen.

TAKE A CLOSER LOOK

What will happen if we don't take time to listen to the stories our loved ones have about the past? We learn from the past, so if we do not listen, we may make similar mistakes from the past. We could forget important events from our community's past.

Ask your instructor or a loved one about a story from their past that is important to them. Did the story teach you something? What happened in the story?

WRITE

What is the purpose of a timeline?

....

....

....

....

....

....

....

READ

Identifying Past, Present, and Future

How can we tell if an event is in the past, present, or future? Timelines are one tool we can use. A timeline has a title, the date, and the event. The date tells you when the event happened, and the events are in order.

There are other ways to tell if something is past, present, and future. Geologists study layers of rock to guess how old something is. The oldest layer of rock is at the bottom, and the higher layers are newer. The top layer, where we walk, is what is happening in the present.

HOW DOES GEOLOGY TEACH ABOUT THE PAST?

We can learn a lot about what happened before we were born in the different layers of rocks. In those layers are fossils of bones and items, which helps us learn about that time. Geologists looking at these layers learn about dinosaurs who lived long ago before humans walked the Earth.

Another example of geology teaching us about the past is at the former city Pompeii. Pompeii is an archaeological site in southern Italy. Once a flourishing Roman city, Pompeii was buried in ash after the eruption of Mount Vesuvius in 79 AD. This ash preserved the city, and it is now a time capsule for what life was like in ancient Rome. A geologist can now study this area to learn about the past.

WRITE

How do we use rock layers to learn about the past?

....
....
....
....
....

Pompeii

Pompeii is a preserved ancient Roman city in Campania, Italy. On August 24, 79 AD, a massive eruption from Mount Vesuvius showered volcanic debris over Pompeii. For many centuries, Pompeii stayed beneath the ash, until it was unearthed in the 1700s. Today you can visit the ruins, which are still being studied and excavated.

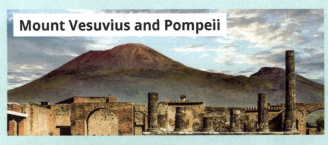

Mount Vesuvius and Pompeii

ruins of a temple in Pompeii

PRACTICE

Create a timeline of your life or a historical figure's life. The timeline should include five major events, dates, pictures, and a title. The events should be in chronological order. Here is an example of a timeline of Malala Yousafzai, who is an activist from Pakistan. She defied the Taliban in Pakistan and demanded that girls be allowed to receive an education. Notice that the oldest event (Malala's birth) is first in the timeline. The most recent event (Malala winning the Nobel Peace Prize) is last.

Malala Yousafzai Timeline

July 12, 1997	July 2008	October 9, 2012	October 9, 2013	October 10, 2014
Malala Yousafzai was born.	Malala gave her first speech about how the Taliban didn't allow females to get an education	The Taliban attempted to assassinate Malala.	Malala's memoir, "I Am Malala" is released.	Malala wins the Nobel Peace Prize.

Draw your timeline in the box below.

REVIEW

In this lesson, you learned:

- The past is what already happened. The present is what is happening now. The future is what will happen.

- Timelines and geology are tools used to determine whether something is past, present, or future.

Think About It

Who is someone in your family that might have stories you don't know about? Why is it important that we hear them?

Match the vocabulary word to the correct definition.

VOCABULARY	DEFINITION

VOCABULARY

1. _____ past

2. _____ present

3. _____ future

4. _____ primary source

5. _____ secondary source

6. _____ timeline

7. _____ chronological

DEFINITION

A. the time happening right now

B. a display of events that have happened chronologically

C. the order of events

D. the time that has not happened yet

E. any time that has already happened

F. written after the event has taken place

G. accounts from people who witnessed the events

8. How can geology teach us about the past? Circle all correct answers.

A. The rock layers can tell us the order of events.

B. The rocks can talk to us about what they have seen.

C. Earth can preserve the past like in Pompeii.

D. Geology does not help us learn about the past.

TAKE A CLOSER LOOK

Through time some items that used to be helpful are now no longer needed because we found a better way to do things. When an item is no longer required to help us, we call that becoming obsolete. An example of this is movie rental stores. Before online streaming, people would go check out movies from a movie rental store. These stores worked like a library, but you had to pay to rent the movies.

What do you think is something we use now that could be obsolete in the future?

Put the milestones of the bike in chronological order on the timeline by adding the sentence's number in the boxes.

9. In 1866, the high-wheeler bike was invented.

10. In 1869, rubber was put on the bike wheels and there was the first bicycle road race.

11. In 1817, the first bike was invented.

12. In 1989, the first helmet laws in the world came out in Australia.

13. In the 1920s, bike companies began making kid bikes.

Lesson 46

Primary and Secondary Sources

By the end of this lesson, you will be able to:

- explain the difference between primary and secondary sources
- identify how primary and secondary sources help us learn about history

Lesson Review

If you need to review the past, present, and future, please go to the lesson titled "Past, Present, Future."

Academic Vocabulary

Read the following vocabulary words and definitions. Look through the lesson. Can you find each vocabulary word? Underline the vocabulary word in your lesson. Write the page number of where you found each word in the blanks.

- **primary source:** accounts from people who witnessed the events (page ____)
- **secondary source:** written after the event has taken place (page ____)

CREATE

Imagine 100 years in the future, a historian finds your journal where you wrote about current events. The journal would be helpful for the historian to learn about what happened in the past. Your journal would be a primary source to the historian. A primary source is an account of events from people who witnessed the event. Create a journal entry discussing a current event. How does this event make you feel? What do you think will happen? Include these in your entry.

....

....

....

....

....

....

....

....

We learn about the past by reading accounts from the past. People in the past wrote in diaries, published newspapers, and took pictures, which were all first-hand accounts about the past. These accounts teach us about a different time. We call these documents **primary sources**. Some examples of primary sources are music, art, journals, recordings, and photographs.

Primary documents give people the ability to peek into the past. Primary sources are valuable because they are our only way to go back into history and learn about the past. Documenting the past is important because, as we have learned in previous lessons, learning from the past helps our society grow and develop.

What are the primary sources in your house? These could be home videos, photo albums, journals, and art. Create a list of the primary sources you find. Try to find at least five examples.

....
....
....
....
....
....
....
....
....

TAKE A CLOSER LOOK

We can also peek into history by looking at photos taken from the event. These photos are pictures taken when Ruby Bridges walked into school for the first day. At the time, schools in the United States were still segregated, and she was the only Black child attending this school.

Six-year-old Ruby Bridges entering school with the marshal.

US Marshals with Young Ruby Bridges on School Steps.jpg by Uncredited DOJ photographer is in the public domain.

Primary and Secondary Sources

Primary sources are told from people who witnessed the event. **Secondary sources** are written after the event has taken place. Examples of primary sources are newspapers, art, and journals. Secondary source examples are history books, documentaries, and nonfiction books. Both sources explain and teach us about the past. Secondary sources and primary sources give us information about history. They differ because primary sources are made during the event, and secondary sources are created after the event.

The photos of Ruby Bridges attending school are a primary source. History books explaining the event are secondary sources. This worktext is a secondary source because it describes the past after it has happened. Can you think of other examples of secondary sources? What do you think will be valuable primary sources in the future? Social media is a primary source. People living through events are describing it through their perspective. In the future, historians can use social media to learn about what life today is like for people.

Quick Tip

How can you tell if a source is credible? Some sources are written by a person who did not research the event well, or they may have a firm opinion and leave out information. An excellent place to find reliable sources is library periodicals. Other sources are websites ending in ".gov" and ".org." Also, when reading the source, ask yourself, "What is the author's purpose? Is the goal to convince, inform, or persuade?" Understanding the perspective can help you know if the information is accurate. It is helpful to look at multiple sources from different perspectives to understand the event better.

What is an example of a primary source? What is an example of a secondary source?

....

....

....

READ

Sources Inform Us About the Past

Primary sources give us a point of view from a person living through the event. We can learn about their feelings about the event and their personal experience. An example is the *Diary of Anne Frank*. Anne wrote about her and her family's account of their two years (1942–1944) in hiding during the German occupation of the Netherlands during World War II. At the time, she was a teenager. Her diary helps us learn about personal experiences during historical events. When historians study the past, they piece together these documents to form an understanding of the past.

Writing about historical events, people, objects, or ideas produce secondary sources because they help explain new or different positions and opinions about primary sources. Secondary sources also give us an overview of events and help show cause and effect. For instance, historians can piece together information from the past to see what led to events. Secondary sources often include primary sources in their writing. They also help explain primary documents.

Statue of Anne Frank in Amsterdam

Both secondary and primary sources are important because they help give us a deep understanding of the past.

WRITE

Why are secondary sources important?

PRACTICE

Fill out the Venn diagram with two differences between primary sources and secondary sources. Also include one similarity between primary sources and secondary sources. Think about how they teach us about history and their importance.

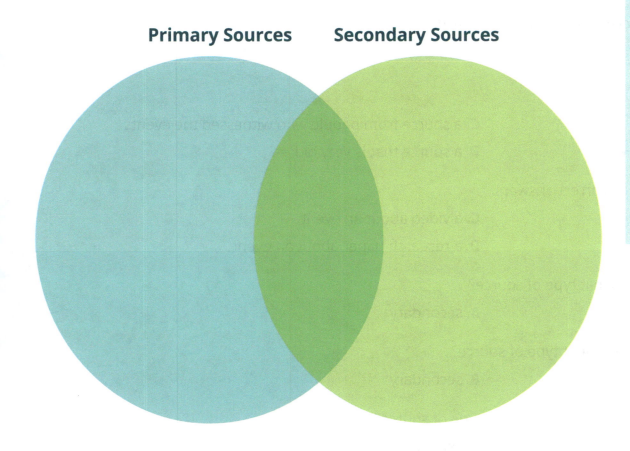

Primary Sources   **Secondary Sources**

REVIEW

In this lesson, you learned:

- Primary sources are sources written by someone involved in an event. Secondary sources are written after an event.

- We learn about the past with primary and secondary sources.

Think About It

Is it important to look at multiple primary sources from different points of view?

Match the document to the correct source.

Sources: Documents:

1. primary source   **A.** The Declaration of Independence

2. secondary source   **B.** *Discover! Social Studies* worktext

Circle the correct answer.

3. A primary source is _____.

    A. a source written after the event   **C.** a source from people who witnessed the events

    B. a source explaining the cause and effect of an event   **D.** a source that is very old

4. What are examples of secondary sources? Circle all correct answers.

    A. a history textbook   **C.** a video about an event

    B. a journal entry   **D.** a research paper about an event

5. An interview with a World War II veteran would be what type of source?

    A. primary   **B.** secondary

6. A History Channel special on ancient China would be what type of source?

    A. primary   **B.** secondary

7. The speech "I Have a Dream" by Martin Luther King Jr. would be what type of source?

    A. primary   **B.** secondary

8. The diary entries of Lewis and Clark would be what type of source?

    A. primary   **B.** secondary

9. How do primary sources teach us about the past?

....
....
....
....
....

10. How do secondary sources teach us about the past?

....
....
....
....
....

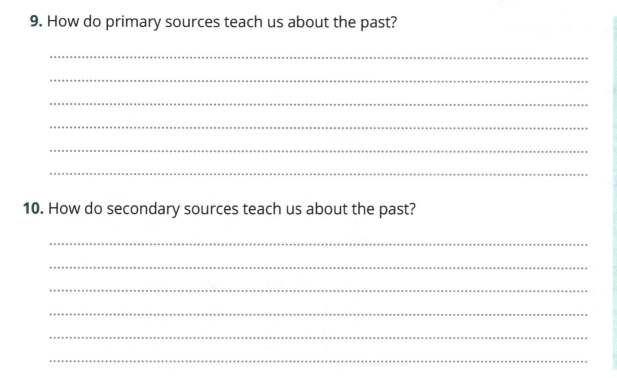

ONLINE CONNECTION

What is something from the past you want to learn about? Have your instructor help you research primary and secondary sources online. Remember to find credible sources. Then create a timeline about the subject you researched. A timeline is a way to organize events in the past in the order in which they happened.

Lesson 47

Global and Historical Communities

By the end of this lesson, you will be able to:

- explain how people in different times and places view the world
- describe global and historical communities

Lesson Review

If you need to review the past and present, please go to the lesson titled "Past, Present, Future."

Academic Vocabulary

Read the following vocabulary words and definitions. Look through the lesson. Can you find each vocabulary word? Underline the vocabulary word in your lesson. Write the page number of where you found each word in the blanks.

- **stewardship:** taking care of something (page ____)
- **worldview:** the way someone thinks about the world (page ____)

CREATE

"Be patient with your enemies and forgiving of your friends," is an Afghan proverb. Around the world, cultures have proverbs, which are pieces of advice. In Christianity, there are many proverbs to help guide the people of the faith. For example, Luke 6:31 says, "Do unto others as you would have them do unto you." Many proverbs illustrate a culture's values. What is a proverb you have heard in your culture or family? Create a picture to illustrate the proverb.

EXPLORE

Did you know that all around the world, people enjoy different foods, holidays, and traditions? Let us take a trip around the world and learn about the various winter holidays people celebrate!

Wat, from Ethiopia

Latkes

Dumplings

In Ethiopia, they celebrate Christmas on January 7, but call it Gaana. They enjoy wat, a thick, spicy stew of meat, vegetables, and sometimes eggs. Children during this time play a game that is a lot like hockey, using a curved stick and a round wooden ball.

In Israel, most people celebrate Hanukkah, the Jewish Festival of Lights. It begins in November or December, depending on the year, and lasts for eight days. During Hanukkah, people enjoy latkes, which are potato pancakes, and jelly doughnuts. Millions of people worldwide who are of the Jewish faith, not just people in Israel, celebrate Hanukkah.

In China, they celebrate the Chinese New Year. It marks the end of winter and is usually around February. Dumplings are a staple in Chinese cuisine related to wealth. According to tradition, the more dumplings you eat during the new year celebrations, the more money you can make in the new year. At the end of the celebration, there is the Lantern Festival.

Worldviews

Worldviews are the way someone thinks about the world. For example, the worldview of Christianity is that there is one God and Jesus is their savior.

The ancient Greeks believed in the Olympic gods, not just one God. The ancient Greeks had many core beliefs such as loyalty, teamwork, and generosity. Today in Greece, people see the Olympic gods as stories, and many now identify as Christian.

Many Indigenous people believe Earth is pure and should be honored. The Cherokee Nation believes in group harmony and freely sharing and giving time and talents. They also value **stewardship** of the land.

The Islamic Golden Age took place during the 8th to 13th centuries. The Golden Age was when science, culture, technology, education, and the arts grew in the Islamic Empire. Islamic people in the past and today believe humans have free will. Also, they believe life should be lived in submission to Allah (God).

Olympic gods and goddesses

What is a view Cherokee people hold?

....

....

....

READ

Global and Historical Communities

A community is a group of people who share something in common. To be a community, you need people who are alike in some way. What makes a community unique is their beliefs, their way of life, and where they live.

India is a diverse place with many communities within it. They have different landscapes too. In India, you can find mountains, flatlands used for farming, and sandy beaches. Many people in India practice Hinduism, a religion. In Hinduism, they believe in a universal soul, or God, called Brahman. Brahman takes on many forms that some Hindus worship as gods or goddesses.

In 700–500 BC, the Celtic Gauls arrived in France. In 58–50 BC, France became part of the Roman Empire, where it remained until 476 AD. Kings ruled the French for many centuries until the French Revolution in 1789. Today, France is a democracy. France is known for its gourmet food and fashion. Most people in France practice Christianity or Islam.

Sámi country stretches across the northern part of Scandinavia and Russia. The traditional Sámi religion believed in many gods and held beliefs connected to the land. They believe that objects, places, and creatures all have a spiritual being. Today many Sámi consider themselves Christian after missionaries came to Scandinavia in the 1720s and converted many.

Sámi brooch

Ganesh is a Hindu god of new beginnings.

Environmental Worldviews

The human-centered view sees humans as the most important species. Different species only have value if they are helpful to humans. The stewardship-based view believes humans should care for Earth. Humans' goal is to take care of nature. The nature-centered view sees all species as equal. Every living thing on the Earth has value.

WRITE

Think about your community. What are the unique aspects of your communities? It could be your faith community, the community you live in, or a community with people who share an interest.

....

....

....

PRACTICE

What is your environmental worldview? Many cultures have different views on how humans should see the Earth's resources. You can be a mix of the other environmental worldviews. Draw and describe how in your perfect world humans would attend to the Earth.

Fill in the blank.

1. _____ is taking care of something like the Earth.

2. The way a person views the world is called _____.

3. What is a community?

   A. People who disagree on many things.

   B. A group of people who share something in common.

   C. A group of people from different regions.

   D. People from different backgrounds.

4. What grew in the Islamic Golden Age? Circle all correct answers.

   A. science

   B. culture

   C. technology

   D. education

5. What are the two main religions in France?

   A. Buddhism and Christianity

   B. Judaism and Islam

   C. Christianity and Islam

   D. They do not have any religions.

6. Write about your community's worldviews. What are the core beliefs where you live?

   ....
   ....
   ....
   ....
   ....

CREATE

Here is an excerpt of an Afghan poem written by Rumi. "Yesterday I was clever, so I wanted to change the world. Today I am wise, so I am changing myself." His view is that to change the world, he must start within. Create your short poem about an aspect of your worldview.

Lesson 48

Perspectives Across Time

By the end of this lesson, you will be able to:

- compare and contrast two or more perspectives from the same place in the world but across different time periods

Lesson Review

If you need to review how places change over time, please go to the lesson titled "Past, Present, Future."

Academic Vocabulary

Read the following vocabulary words and definitions. Look through the lesson. Can you find each vocabulary word? Underline the vocabulary word in your lesson. Write the page number of where you found each word in the blanks.

- **Indigenous people:** the first people to live in an area (page ___)
- **nomad:** a person who moves from place to place and does not settle (page ___)
- **perspective:** a point of view that affects the way you look at or think about things (page ___)

IN THE
REAL WORLD

Have you ever thought one thing, but then changed your mind? Of course! Most people change their minds from time to time. In today's lesson, we will learn how this can happen in a historic place. People can change their points of view over time.

So what happens to make someone change their mind? You may get more information about a topic that changes your understanding. Maybe you had an experience that caused you to feel differently, or someone with a different point of view convinced you to change your mind.

What is something that you have changed your mind about?

Maria, Grace, and Marcus are three friends who live next door to each other. One day, Maria walks outside and notices a cloud of smoke coming from Grace's backyard. She is worried because it looks like the house is on fire!

Maria calls Marcus to ask if he can see anything. Marcus looks out his window and notices the smoke too, but he isn't worried at all. He tells Grace to come over to his house.

When Grace looks at the yard from the same perspective as Marcus, she sees that her idea was incorrect. The smoke is actually coming from a barbecue. Maria could not tell because a fence was blocking her view.

The two witnesses each had a different look at what happened. We can say they had two different **perspectives**. People can have different perspectives on events for many reasons. In this case, Maria did not have the whole story. Other times, people can change their minds over time, causing them to see things differently.

How do we see things from a different perspective? How could people from the same place see things differently? Could people's thoughts about historical events be affected by their point of view? How and why are there different perspectives over time?

From this perspective, it looks like the house may be on fire.

From this perspective, we can see it is a barbecue.

 **READ**

The Indigenous Australians

The **Indigenous** Australians were the first inhabitants of Australia. These first people have lived there for thousands of years and are the world's oldest continuous culture. Many of their traditions are told through stories. They passed down knowledge through storytelling and did not write in books.

They had a spiritual connection to the land and animals that lived in the desert climate of Australia. They lived as **nomads**, without fixed cities or villages. Family groups moved around by season, staying settled only for short periods of time.

The Indigenous people did not think of themselves as land owners. The land was special and their job was to care for it. They managed the wilderness by burning trees and shrubs when they became too large. Waterways were especially important as streams were considered spiritual. They used water from many sources such as rivers, rain, and tree roots so that the creeks never went dry. Men hunted kangaroos and large birds using spears and the boomerang.

WRITE Are the ways of the Indigenous people of Australia different from the customs where you live? Explain two differences.

....

....

....

....

....

....

 **IN THE REAL WORLD**

The Dreaming

The Indigenous Australians believed in a worldview called "The Dreaming." The Australians believed their ancient ancestors breathed life into the natural world. These ancestors then settled as spirits in the physical world. Rocks, trees, and animals contain the spirits of the ancestors from the "Dreamtime." Special rock formations, trees, and animals like the kangaroo, crocodile, or honey ant all contain the spirit and life force from the ancestors.

The Uluru rock formation, a sacred place in the Dreaming

The British Perspective

One way that perspectives can change is when new people come to a place. British people came to Australia in the 1700s. They brought different ideas and a different way of life. The British people did not fully understand or appreciate the culture and ideas of the Indigenous Australians.

The British were used to a system where land was owned by individuals. People stayed in one spot and created a home that was fenced in or had a boundary line. They were used to cities with many people and large buildings. The British recorded laws, rules, and knowledge in books.

When the British looked at the landscape of Australia, they thought it was open and free for them to take over and create their own cities and homes. They did not find books, written documents, or a large government. They thought that the Indigenous people did not have an organized way of life.

For hundreds of years, the British Australians looked down on the Indigenous ideas. The native Australians were often forced to give up their ways and tried to be more like the British. They were forced to learn English, go to British-style schools, and live in cities. The British Australians thought they were improving the Indigenous people. But the native people saw it as losing an entire way of life.

Modern Perspectives

In modern times, most Australians have a new perspective. Most people understand that the events were unjust and sad for the Indigenous people. They realize that the Australian Aboriginal people had a full and rich culture that the British people simply did not understand. Over the last 30 to 40 years, modern Australians have developed a new perspective. The way they were mistreated is now understood to be wrong. Today, the nation makes an effort to recognize and celebrate the culture of Indigenous peoples.

TAKE A CLOSER LOOK

Arrival at Botany Bay

The First Fleet was a group of 11 ships from Britain that landed at Botany Bay in Australia in 1787. The British included many sailors and prisoners who were being released from jail.

Over time, the settlers built fences, farms, and villages. To the Indigenous people, this was disturbing. New people took over the land that they had cared for for thousands of years. The British blocked access to the spiritual waters and changed the balance of the land.

The First Fleet entering Port Jackson, January 26, 1788, drawn 1888 A9333001h.jpg by E. Le Bihan is in the public domain.

WRITE

How did the British idea of owning land conflict with the Indigenous beliefs?

....
....
....
....
....
....
....
....
....
....
....
....
....
....
....
....
....
....
....
....

REVIEW

In this lesson, you learned:

- Not everyone has the same perspective.

- The Indigenous Australians moved around the land and lived in tune with nature.

- British people came to Australia and brought different perspectives with them.

- British Australians looked down on the Indigenous culture and treated people harshly.

- Modern Australians have made efforts to better understand and honor Indigenous culture.

- Perspectives can change over time if new people with new ideas move to an area, or if people gain new understandings or information.

Think About It

How can two peoples with very different ideas work out their differences peacefully?

Circle True or False for each statement.

1. True or False   Indigenous Australians fenced in small pieces of land.

2. True or False   Indigenous Australians believed the spirits lived in rocks, trees, and animals.

3. True or False   The Spanish were the new people who came to Australia.

4. True or False   The British believe that knowledge was passed down in written books.

5. True or False   The British settlers kept the land in a natural state.

Put the events in the order they happened. Number them from 1–5 starting with the first event. Write the correct number in the blank.

6. _____ The British sailed to Australia.

7. _____ Native Australians established a way of life that respects nature.

8. _____ The British think that Australia is unclaimed, so they take over.

9. _____ Australians promote respect for the Indigenous people.

10. _____ Indigenous Australians were forced to be more like the British people.

11. How did the Indigenous Australians and the British see things differently? Give two examples.

....

....

....

ONLINE CONNECTION

Australian Arts
New perspectives in Australia are leading to a better appreciation of the Indigenous way of life. Let's learn more about their rich culture. Use the internet to research the arts of the native Australian people. Find examples of the following art styles:

· Australian dot-art

· Didgeridoo music

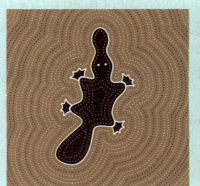 

Perspective Across Places

By the end of this lesson, you will be able to:

- compare and contrast two or more perspectives from different places in the world during the same time period

Lesson Review

If you need to review how different people have different governments, please go to the lesson titled "Forms of Government."

Academic Vocabulary

Read the following vocabulary words and definitions. Look through the lesson. Can you find each vocabulary word? Underline the vocabulary word in your lesson. Write the page number of where you found each word in the blanks.

- **debate:** a discussion of different viewpoints on a topic (page ____)

- **democracy:** a type of government ruled by the citizens (page ____)

- **legalism:** a type of government that uses laws and harsh punishment to keep order and control people (page ____)

- **perspective:** a point of view that affects the way you look at or think about things (page ____)

- **Taoism:** a Chinese philosophy that seeks to live in balance with nature (page ____)

CREATE

In this lesson, you will learn about different perspectives on government in ancient Athens and China. Use poster paper to create a K–W–L chart. Divide the paper into three sections and label them K, W, and L. You can record what you already Know, what you Want to learn, and what you did Learn after the lesson. Begin by writing in the K section what you already know about China, Athens, and governments. Then list three to five questions you have about these topics in the W section. Finally, when the lesson is over, write the most important things you have learned in the L section.

When people live together in communities, they must decide between two different important concepts. On one side, communities need laws and rules so that everyone can live together and get along. On the other hand, most people want to be free to live their life however they wish. Many people want to have a say in their government and make decisions about how their own community or country is run.

This is a balancing act that people have thought about for thousands of years. Some places have very powerful leaders, such as a king or emperor. Sometimes they have very harsh laws to make sure people follow the leader's ideas, while other places think that the common people should be able to make decisions for themselves. Remember that we learned that people have different **perspectives**, or points of view.

Do you think people in different parts of the world may have different views about government? What could cause people to develop different perspectives?

....
....
....
....
....
....
....
....
....
....
....

You are going to learn about perspectives from Greece and China. Here you can see the location of these nations on the map. They are over 4,000 miles (6,400 kilometers) away from each other! When people live far away, they can often have different ideas and experiences.

Athens

Let's look back in time to Athens, Greece. The time period is about 400 BC—over 2,000 years ago! Though this is long ago, the point of view that started here is still very important today.

Citizens in Athens discuss ideas for the city.

Cities in Greece were isolated from each other. Each town operated just like its own small country. Some of the cities were led by rich, powerful people. They told everyone else what to do. But in Athens, citizens wanted to make things fairer and give everyone some power. Athenians believed that common people could make decisions for themselves. Everyone could work together to figure out how to build a great city to live in.

They decided on a system called **democracy**. In this system, everyone would have a say in the government through voting. People were allowed to select leaders who would represent their best interests. The people of Athens even voted on laws and rules for the city. Lots of different people took turns being leaders in the city.

The idea of democracy is based on the point of view that all citizens should be given equal value. The government leaders were supposed to serve the people. They believed that by giving everyone the freedom to come up with ideas and vote, the city would constantly improve.

Quick Tip

Remember what we learned about perspective in the last lesson? Perspectives can change over time. The democracy that started in Athens did not truly represent everyone. For example, only men could be citizens. Women were not allowed to participate in the government at all.

But over time, people learned that this was not fair. They changed their point of view. Modern democracies now better hold to the principles that were started in Athens. Women vote and hold leadership positions in democracies all across the world.

WRITE

The ideas of Athens have impacted many governments today. Do any of these ideas sound similar to the government where you live?

....

....

....

....

....

Legalism

At this same time, thinkers in China came to a different answer to the question of how the government should work. The idea of legalism influenced their government. In **legalism**, having strict rules that keep everything orderly is a primary goal.

In Athens, people got involved by voting and serving in the government. In China, people had a different **perspective**. They felt that the country would operate best if only the emperor and other powerful advisors made decisions. Everyone did their part to make the Chinese nation more powerful and support the leaders.

Chinese leaders believed that ordinary people could not be trusted. China enacted a strict law code. The leader appointed trusted ministers to oversee parts of the country and make sure everyone followed the emperor's rules. People could not question or disobey the leaders.

Protecting the ideas and rights of each individual person was not the goal of the government. Most people spent their time working hard to make China more powerful and wealthy. They farmed crops for food or made silk to be sold. Many men worked to build government structures such as the Great Wall of China.

Legalist leaders believed that a country worked best when all the power was centered on a single powerful leader and his advisors. That way, all of China would follow a single set of rules and plans. The common people would do their part to support the leaders and make China more powerful. The overall success of China as a country was more important than giving people power.

TAKE A CLOSER LOOK

Some thinkers in China did not think that legalism had all the answers. They thought it was unnatural to make so many laws. The leader of this group was Lao Tzu. Lao Tzu's teachings formed a way of life called Taoism. Taoists see people as part of the natural way of the universal force, called the Tao.

From his perspective, people should live a balanced life with nature. Lao Tzu wanted people to avoid conflicts. He advised people to find a way around problems and not to try to convince others of their own ideas.

READ

Comparing Perspectives

Let's think about some examples of how people with different perspectives may come to different conclusions. People with different perspectives will see the same thing differently. They are not necessarily "right" or "wrong." They just see things in a different way.

In Athens, citizens often debated. A **debate** is a discussion about a topic where each side tries to convince the other they are correct. Whenever a new idea was proposed, Athenians would debate and argue to decide whether it was a good idea. Citizens felt that by arguing both sides, they could come to the best decision. Debate is still a common practice in democracies today.

But in China, questioning a law was forbidden. Citizens were supposed to support the leader and the law. Legalists thought that debate was dangerous to the country and could even put people in prison. The emperor and his ministers were the only ones trusted to make decisions, and everyone was to follow without question.

Because of their different points of view, people in Athens and China created completely different perspectives on government.

REVIEW

In this lesson, you learned:

- People in different places can have different points of view in the same time period.
- Athenians believed that all citizens should be able to have a say in the government.
- Athenians believed that the government should work to promote individuals.
- In China, Legalists believed that people should be controlled by harsh laws and punishment.
- Taoists thought people should be most concerned with living in harmony with nature.

Think About It

Is voting always good? What could go wrong with majority rule?

Do you think legalism helped unify China?

Show **WHAT YOU KNOW**

Fill in the blank with a word from the Word Bank.

Word Bank: Athens   China   London   nature   voting
          wealth   punishment   rights

1. The city of _____ started the idea of democracy.

2. Leaders of Athens were selected by _____.

3. Legalism was an idea started in ancient _____.

4. Legalists believed in harsh _____.

5. Lao Tzu taught people to live in harmony with _____.

ONLINE CONNECTION

Use an online search to find out more about Emperor Shi–Huang–Di. He was considered the strongest of all Legalist leaders. He wanted to unify and protect China. Some of his accomplishments were very important. However, other ideas harmed the common people. Make a list of both his positive and negative actions.

Circle the correct answer.

6. True or False   Democracy started in the United States of America.

7. True or False   Leaders of Athens were chosen by voting.

8. True or False   Legalists did not trust the people to make their own decisions.

9. True or False   Legalists thought common people should work to make China powerful.

10. True or False   Taoists stressed living in harmony with nature.

11. Compare the perspectives of ancient Athens and ancient China. What are two differences in their points of view about government?

....
....
....

Lesson 50

Culture and Ethnicity

By the end of this lesson, you will be able to:

- identify the elements of culture and ethnicity
- describe the important elements of at least two distinct cultures

Lesson Review

If you need to review how people in different places have different ways of life, please go to the lesson titled "Global and Historical Communities."

Academic Vocabulary

Read the following vocabulary words and definitions. Look through the lesson. Can you find each vocabulary word? Underline the vocabulary word in your lesson. Write the page number of where you found each word in the blanks.

- **culture:** all the beliefs, ways of life, and arts passed down by a group of people (page ____)
- **ethnicity:** a group of people who identify together because of shared history and culture (page ____)
- **pastoralist:** people who raise grazing animals in large outdoor grasslands (page ____)

Learn About Your Culture

In this lesson, you will learn about different cultures—all the beliefs, ways of life, and arts passed down by a group of people. Do you know what culture your ancestors came from? You can interview family members to find out.

As you complete the lesson, you can also research your own culture and make comparisons to the ones you will learn about today. Work with your instructor to research the traditional parts of your cultural background, including:

- Language
- Food
- Clothing
- Religion
- Art
- Music

In many cities, ethnic groups form small neighborhoods with people from the same place who have a similar way of life. A group's **ethnicity** is based on their shared history and culture.

Each group brings their own unique culture or way of life. **Culture** is made up of many things, including language, religious beliefs, art, music, and food.

One example of a small, ethnic neighborhood in New York is Little Italy. Here, there are many restaurants with Italian specialties. Some of the people will speak the Italian language. Visiting Little Italy may make you feel a little bit like you are in another country.

What characteristics do people in these ethnic neighborhoods share?

Why do you think immigrants may settle near others from their ethnic group?

....
....
....
....
....
....
....
....

IN THE REAL WORLD

People from China have moved to many places around the world. Many large western cities have "Chinatowns." Many of these immigrants have kept elements of their traditional culture.

What would you experience in Chinatown?

You will see Chinese-style buildings and clothing. Visitors can smell the cooking of Chinese foods. Residents often speak in Chinese languages such as Mandarin or Cantonese.

Here you can experience elements of Chinese culture.

Entering Chinatown in Washington, DC

READ

Life in Japan

Japan is a country in Asia made up of several islands. The nation is highly unified and has a strong national culture.! Let's examine some of the characteristics of the Japanese way of life.

Japanese citizens often value hard work and respect for authority figures. People usually try to honor the leader of the family or their boss at work. Because of their hard work, business and technology have made Japan a recognized leader in technology.

Although the Japanese are successful in modern industry, respect for tradition is important.

An example is the tea ceremony. People gather for a special ceremony to prepare and drink green matcha tea. They dress in traditional clothing such as the kimono, a wrapped clothing made with beautiful colors.

The Japanese also have many arts and pastimes in their culture. Japanese artists work with ceramics, painting, and animation.

Yōshū Chikanobu Cha no yu.jpg by Yōshū Chikanobu is in the public domain.

TAKE A CLOSER LOOK

Thirty-Six Views of Mount Fuji

Here you see one of the paintings from the series *Thirty-Six Views of Mount Fuji*. This shows a large and dangerous wave with a large mountain in the background. Woodblock prints showing nature are common in Japanese art.

It is no surprise that Mt. Fuji was a common subject in art. The large mountain is a spiritual center for the Japanese Shinto religion.

Great Wave off Kanagawa2.jpg by Katsushika Hokusai is in the public domain.

The Maasai

The Maasai are an ethnic group who live in East Africa. They inhabit the grassland areas of Kenya and Tanzania. They traditionally live in small villages made up of four to ten families. Most Maasai speak their traditional Maa language and the regional language of Swahili.

You can often recognize the Maasai because of their vibrant red clothing.

The Maasai live a way of life based on **pastoralism**. They are expert herders who keep flocks of sheep and herds of cows. Rather than establishing a farm in one area, the Maasai move around with the cattle based on natural patterns. The cows move around each season to find the best location for grass and water. The Maasai families move with them, setting up a temporary shelter to live in. They get everything they need from the cows. They drink milk and eat beef as their main source of food.

The Maasai also create intricate and beautiful art. Jewelry made from beadwork is very popular with tourists.

READ

Comparing Cultures

Human beings have many things in common. They all need food and shelter. They express themselves with clothing, art, and music. They have languages to communicate. However, these are also the differences in each ethnic group's culture.

PRACTICE

1. True or False   Japanese people live only in small villages.

2. True or False   The Maasai people live in Africa.

3. True or False   Mt. Fuji is a holy place to the Japanese.

4. True or False   The Maasai traditionally drink tea.

5. True or False   The most important animal to the Maasai is the pig.

REVIEW

In this lesson, you learned:

- A people with a shared history and way of life is an ethnic group.
- A people's traditions, customs, language, and arts make up their culture.
- In some places, such as New York, many ethnic groups live close together.
- The Japanese have a strong, unified culture.
- The Maasai live a pastoralist life in Africa.

Think About It

Are there any strong cultural or ethnic traditions that are passed down in your family?

Fill in the blank with a word from the Word Bank.

Word Bank: Asia Africa pork tea beef fish pastoralists farmer
ocean culture ethnic group

1. _____ is all the beliefs, ways of life, and arts passed down by a group of people.

2. Japanese people celebrate the _____ ceremony.

3. Rice and _____ are the main foods in Japan.

4. The Maasai live in eastern _____.

5. The Maasai are _____, people who raise grazing animals in large outdoor grasslands.

Answer the following question in complete sentences.

6. Compare Japanese arts to Maasai arts. What are several examples of each?

....

....

....

....

....

....

....

....

Kenya and Japan

Here you can see the location of Kenya and Japan on the world map. Find your own home country on the map. Are you located near or far from the Japanese and Maasai?

Lesson 51

Comparing Cultures

By the end of this lesson, you will be able to:

- compare both the similarities and differences between different cultures with an emphasis on accepting and understanding why these differences exist
- identify and describe how conflict among groups and organizations have impacted history

Lesson Review

If you need to review what a culture is, please go to the lesson titled "Culture and Ethnicity."

Academic Vocabulary

Read the following vocabulary words and definitions. Look through the lesson. Can you find each vocabulary word? Underline the vocabulary word in your lesson. Write the page number of where you found each word in the blanks.

- **culture:** all the beliefs, ways of life, and arts passed down by a group of people (page ___)
- **custom:** a practice common to a culture (page ___)
- **ethnicity:** a group of people who identify together because of shared history and culture (page ___)
- **settle:** to form a community (page ___)

Special Family Practices

Does your family have special holidays for which they dress up for? Or do your relatives cook special foods when celebrating a certain holiday?

Research to find out where your special family practice came from. Be prepared to share your family's special practice with the class.

....
....
....
....

EXPLORE

Our culture defines who we are. It is special to us and unique to our family. Families have special bonds and share a culture. We all have this in common with other family groups: a sense of closeness and fondness.

Unfortunately, sometimes serious disagreements and conflicts arise between different cultures. However, if we learn to understand and recognize how we are more alike than different we will find a new appreciation for our fellow world citizens.

Win-win solutions are the best. Everyone is left feeling their views and concerns are heard and addressed. Also, having compassion for others helps us to remember we are more alike than different.

How do you think a win-win compromise and compassion will help people to work together?

IN THE REAL WORLD

Research to find out how to say *thank you* in various languages.

What Is Culture?

Culture is all the beliefs, ways of life, and arts passed down by a group of people. Culture describes many things, like language, food, clothing, music, arts, customs, and beliefs. **Ethnicity** means a person's cultural background. An ethnic group is a group of people who identify together because of shared history and culture

Humans have evolved over time and developed different cultures. The environment where people live helps to decide their culture. Remember, culture represents a way of life. For example, a group of people that **settle**, or form a community, in a cold and mountainous region of the world would develop a different culture from a group of people who settle in a hot and dry desert region.

We should respect and celebrate the differences in all people. We can learn new and exciting things when we are open to learning about others and their differences. There are lots of things we have in common with other people, even if we have different cultures. Someone who looks different from you might have the same interests as you.

How would you describe your culture? Describe your language, food, clothing, music, arts, customs, and beliefs. Do you know anyone with a cultural background different from yours? How are you alike and how are you different?

....
....
....
....

Cultural Foods

All people eat. However, culture changes what and how people eat. For example, in China, people eat a lot of rice because the conditions are good for growing rice. They eat rice as a side dish or as part of a main dish. In Mexico, the main crop grown is corn. Mexico has a variety of dishes using corn.

A custom is a practice common to a culture. Most Americans use forks when eating. In Japan, people commonly use chopsticks to eat. In the United States, food is served on plates and in bowls. In some parts of India, food is served on banana leaves.

What food does your family eat a lot of? How does your family eat?

READ

The Arab–Israeli Conflict

The Arab–Israeli conflict is a term used to describe the political pressures and open fighting between the Arab countries of the Middle East and North Africa and the State of Israel. The conflict has been ongoing since 1948.

Political movements tend to instigate disagreements and conflicts among different cultures. This is the reason that the Arab-Israeli conflict began between the Arab and Jewish people in the Middle East and North Africa and the State of Israel. The rise of the Zionist movement among the Jews and the Palestinian Arab nationalism instigated conflict among these cultures.

The area where the conflict arose between these cultural groups was called Mandatory Palestine. There were disagreements about who owned the land there. The Jewish people saw this place as their historical homeland otherwise called the Land of Israel. However, the Palestinian Arab movement saw this region as belonging to them.

There have been various wars and takeovers by these two groups through the years. This cultural disagreement around land ownership has changed from the large-scale Arab–Israeli conflict to a more local Israeli-Palestinian struggle, though the Arab World and Israel still disagree with each other over specific territory.

ONLINE CONNECTION

Make a timeline of events that have happened related to the Jewish and Palestinian cultural conflict. Imagine you are a peacekeeper. What suggestion would you make for these cultural groups to try to find agreement?

WRITE

What is the reason the cultural struggle between the Jews and the Palestinians is still happening today?

....

....

....

....

....

....

The War of 1812

The War of 1812 was a clash between the United States and the United Kingdom. The United Kingdom was mad at France. They did not want anyone trading with France including the United States. This is the reason why the United Kingdom placed trade restrictions against the United States.

The United Kingdom even captured US trade ships and forced the sailors to join the Royal Navy. To strengthen their cause, the United Kingdom even sided with the Native Americans over white Americans. The United Kingdom did this to keep white Americans from expanding to the west. These actions of force and disagreements led up to and caused the War of 1812.

WRITE

What caused the War of 1812?

....

....

....

REVIEW

In this lesson, you learned:

- Everyone has culture. Every culture has similarities and differences.

- Some cultural differences have impacted various regions of the world.

Think About It

Imagine you make a new friend from a different culture. They may be wearing different clothing or eating different food. How can you make them feel welcomed even though their culture is different?

Match the definition with the correct word.

1. ____ culture

    A. to form a community

2. ____ custom

    B. a group of people who identify together because of shared history and culture

3. ____ ethnicity

    C. a practice common to a culture

4. ____ settle

    D. all the beliefs, ways of life, and arts passed down by a group of people

Read each sentence. Circle True or False.

5. True or False   Language, tools, and food are some of the things that make up a person's culture.

6. True or False   The environment where people live helps to make up their culture.

7. True or False   Sometimes there are cultural disagreements around land use.

8. True or False   Sometimes different cultures use different tools to eat.

CREATE

Pick a culture different from your own that you admire. How is it similar to your culture? How is it different? Create a poster to share the information.

Cooperation Among Groups and Organizations

By the end of this lesson, you will be able to:

- describe how cooperation among groups and organizations has impacted history
- describe how people and places interact and connect in the world

Lesson Review

If you need to review how cultures are different and similar, please go to the lesson titled "Comparing Cultures."

Academic Vocabulary

Read the following vocabulary words and definitions. Look through the lesson. Can you find each vocabulary word? Underline the vocabulary word in your lesson. Write the page number of where you found each word in the blanks.

- **border:** a real line represented on a map and government records that separates geographic areas (page ____)

- **diplomacy:** maintaining peaceful relationships without the use of violence (page ____)

- **incorporation:** the process by which a community seeks to create their own city (page ____)

ONLINE CONNECTION

The goods and services transferred on ships and planes around the globe link us to other people around the world. Companies manufacture the goods and services. Many companies, like Apple, Nike, and McDonald's, operate businesses in more than one country. These types of companies are known as multinational companies. Research a multinational company online. Where is their headquarters? What other countries do they operate in? What goods or services do they provide?

....

....

....

....

EXPLORE

The people of Scotland work together to create a thriving country. As you can see on the map, much of Scotland is surrounded by water. Scotland is known for its wonderful salmon. They export the fish to many countries in the European Union. Use the legend on the map to find other valuable resources in Scotland.

IN THE REAL WORLD

Technology has helped offer new opportunities to make connections. We can make connections with people on the opposite side of the world in a quick manner. For example, someone who lives in Europe can easily message and chat with someone who lives in North America. New technology has made talking to people far away easier!

Before there were cell phones and computers, how do you think people communicated with people who lived far away? How does technology give you the opportunity to exchange ideas and opinions with other people? Talk to your instructor about your answers.

Many people have fought over who owns the resources and where borders should be. Why do you think people on one side of a border wanted the resources belonging to the other side?

....
....
....
....
....

READ

Diplomacy and Disputes

Different groups of people frequently come into conflict when a problem cannot be resolved, when values clash, or when there is uncertainty over ownership of land and resources. In the last lesson, you learned about the conflict between the Jewish and Palestinian people in the Middle East. That conflict began in 1948 and is still ongoing today. **Diplomacy** describes a way of maintaining peaceful relationships without using violence. Diplomacy can help turn a conflict into cooperation.

A **border** is a real line represented on a map and government records that separate geographic areas. Borders are political boundaries. They separate neighborhoods, states, cities, towns, and countries.

A border shows the perimeter of the area in which a particular government has control. The government or governing body of a neighborhood, state, city, town, or country can only create and enforce laws within its borders.

Throughout history, many borders have changed. Sometimes this change has been through cooperation, and other times it has been by force. The peaceful manners involve negotiation and trade. Unfortunately, many times land disputes are not resolved until after a war has taken place. After the war, the decision about who owns the land is decided through international agreements.

TAKE A CLOSER LOOK

Boundaries between places can be vague. A region is a detailed area that has common features. A region can be based on language, government, religion, type of landscape, or climate. Regions can be large areas like the Rocky Mountain National Park or small areas like your favorite park or even your bedroom!

WRITE

What is a border?

READ

Reasons for Land Disputes

Sometimes borders happen to be located along natural boundaries like rivers or mountain ranges. Border disputes can happen as communities seek to create their own cities. This process is called **incorporation**. Many rural or suburban residents fight against incorporation. They prefer to be an unincorporated part of a county instead of part of a town or city. They believe it will lead to more taxes and government rules. Other residents support incorporation and setting their own borders. They say incorporating as a town or city will allow them to have more city services like police, fire, and water and more independence on issues of law enforcement, education, and land use.

One land dispute example was between Mexico and the state of Texas. The border between the two regions follows the Rio Grande River. There was conflict about where the actual border was due to map confusion. Mexico and Texas fought each other for years about this, and the disagreement was not resolved until 1963.

However, not all neighboring countries have border disputes. Canada and the United States, for example, share the world's longest unprotected border, stretching 3,987 miles (6416.46 km).

ONLINE CONNECTION

With the help of an adult, research to find out about a border dispute that has happened in your city or county. Write a report about the dispute. When did this happen, why was there a disagreement, and how was it resolved?

WRITE

Why do people and governments care about borders so much?

....
....
....
....
....

People and Places

A place is somewhere that you identify with. This place has special meaning for you. For example, parts of Earth are identified by special names, like your city's name. However, a place can be as small as your bedroom.

No place exists alone. Not even a rock or a sandbox. Everything is interconnected. Where you live is connected to your neighbor, and the road you live on may connect with other neighborhoods in the area. Our entire world is connected!

We can understand places and interconnection by understanding the purpose of a place. For example, places of worship such as churches and synagogues are connected to people and our world through our spiritual or religious beliefs. Government buildings such as police stations and courthouses are connected to people and our community through their function to support and protect the citizens. The White House and Parliament are connected to one another as they are examples of places that represent our world leaders. Our world leaders are connected to us because citizens vote them in to represent and protect their respective countries.

Classifying places helps us better understand how they are interconnected to each other, to us, and within our world.

REVIEW

In this lesson, you learned:

- A border separates states, cities, countries, and neighborhoods.
- Major disputes have happened over border disagreements.
- Everything is interconnected, including people, places, and things, and all are connected to our world.

Think About It

Have you and your siblings or friends at school ever had a dispute about your space or room boundaries? How did you resolve this issue?

WRITE Think about the places in your community. How do they connect to you? How do they support the citizens in your city?

....

....

....

Match each vocabulary word to the correct definition.

1. _____border

2. _____diplomacy

3. _____incorporation

A. maintaining peaceful relationships without the use of violence

B. the process by which a community seeks to create their own city

C. a real line represented on a map and government records that separates geographic areas

Circle the correct answer.

4. True or False   Diplomacy can help turn a conflict into cooperation.

5. True or False   Throughout history, many borders have changed.

6. True or False   Land shifts throughout time have caused some borders to change.

7. True or False   A place can be as small as your bedroom.

CREATE

What is your favorite place? Draw a picture of this place. Write the name of this place on the picture. Why is it special? How is this place connected to you?

Lesson 53

Chapter 10 Review

By the end of this lesson, you will:

- review the information from the lessons in Chapter 10, "World History."

Lesson Review

Throughout the chapter, we have learned the following big ideas:

- Timelines and other graphic representations can be used to distinguish between past, present, and future. (Lesson 45)
- Primary and secondary sources help us learn about history. (Lesson 46)
- Global and historical communities have impacted our way of life. (Lesson 47)
- Perspectives from the same place in the world but across different time periods have similarities and differences. (Lessons 48 and 49)
- Elements of culture and ethnicity can be identified. Cultures are distinctive and can be described by specific elements. (Lesson 50)
- Conflict among groups and organizations has impacted history. (Lesson 51)
- Cooperation among groups and organizations has impacted history. (Lesson 52)

Go back and review the lessons as needed while you complete the activities.

ONLINE CONNECTION

There are many great resources online with ideas on how to learn about, accept, and understand different cultures.

With an adult's help, look online and see if you can find examples of how people can show acceptance and understanding of different cultures.

Take note of how people will feel if others show them acceptance and understanding.

REVIEW

Indigenous People

The Indigenous people of Australia were content with their lives for many years. However, when the British started settling on their land and changing the process of doing things, they were forced to change. The arrival of a new culture to a place changes the perspectives of everyone involved.

Culture and Ethnicity

Elements of culture and ethnicity can be identified. For example, characteristics of likeness in skin color, language, religions, and customs are things commonly shared by people of the same ethnic background. However, a group of people sharing the same ethnic group oftentimes share the same culture. But shared culture goes beyond likeness in physical appearance. A group of people can have the same culture if they share the same beliefs, rules of conduct, and values.

WRITE — Think of another community or culture that had a changed viewpoint because new people came to their land. How was everyone's perspective impacted?

....
....
....
....
....

What are elements of culture and ethnicity in your family that can be identified? Write about them below.

....
....
....
....

REVIEW

How Conflict Impacted History

The story of the founding of Texas represents one way in which conflict among groups has impacted history. Texas has always been a popular place. Three countries, Spain, France, and America, all at one time laid claim to Texas in the early 1800s. Over the next 30 years, Mexico gained control of Texas even though thousands of American immigrants had settled in the region.

The American immigrants eventually fought against Mexico in 1835. Between 1835 and 1846, the independence that Texas gained for itself allowed for Texas to call itself the Republic of Texas. However, in 1846 it became a state in the United States. Now the argument was focused on the boundary. Mexico and Texas argued over where the border between Mexico and Texas should be. These arguments led to war in 1846. The war lasted two years.

American forces won against Mexico. Their win added present-day New Mexico, Arizona, southern California, parts of Texas, and other areas to the southwest United States. The United States Army showed itself as a mighty force. This conflict has greatly impacted the history of the United States and its citizens' lives to this day. The United States gained the new land and cultural influences of people who lived on these lands, and these effects continue to influence life in the United States today.

Helpful Hints

Here are some helpful tips to think about the big ideas from this chapter:

- We can use timelines and other geographic representations to distinguish between past, present, and future.

- People and places interact and connect in the world.

- Conflict among groups and organizations have impacted history.

- There are similarities and differences between different cultures.

WRITE

Write about a way that a conflict in the past has influenced or impacted you or your country.

....

....

....

....

....

PRACTICE

Vocabulary Memory Game

Using the vocabulary words below, write each term on an index card. On a second index card, write the definition. Shuffle the index cards and line them up face down like the game Memory. Taking turns, flip one of the cards over and locate its respective definition by flipping another card. The person with the most matches wins!

- **border:** a line represented on a map that separates geographic areas
- **chronological:** the order of events
- **culture:** all the consistent beliefs, ways of life, and arts passed down by a group of people
- **custom:** a practice common to a culture
- **debate:** a discussion of different viewpoints on a topic
- **democracy:** a type of government ruled by the citizens
- **diplomacy:** maintaining peaceful relationships without the use of violence
- **ethnicity:** a group of people who identify together because of shared history and culture
- **future:** the time that has not happened yet
- **incorporation:** the process by which communities seek to create their own city
- **Indigenous people:** the first people to live in a particular place
- **legalism:** a type of government that uses laws and harsh punishment to keep order and control people
- **nomad:** a person who moves from place to place and does not settle
- **past:** any time that has already happened
- **pastoralist:** people who raise grazing animals in large outdoor grasslands
- **perspective:** a point of view that affects the way you look at or think about things
- **present:** the time happening right now

Word Study

One way to remember your vocabulary words and their definitions is to draw the meaning of what each vocabulary word represents. For example, for the word *consensus*, you could draw two people shaking hands to represent they have come to an agreement.

- **primary source:** an account from people who witnessed the events
- **secondary source:** an account written after the event has taken place
- **settle:** to form a community
- **Taoism:** a Chinese philosophy that seeks to live in balance with nature
- **timeline:** a visual display of events that have happened chronologically

PRACTICE

Indigenous Culture

Think of an Indigenous culture that you learned about. Describe the culture by writing about their characteristics, customs, and the geography of where they live.

Did this culture experience disagreements with other cultures? If so, write about it. Did this culture experience land disputes? If so, write about it. How was the dispute resolved?

....

....

....

....

....

....

....

....

....

....

....

....

....

....

....

....

....

....

REVIEW

Words like *culture* and *ethnicity* are sometimes used interchangeably. There seems to be some confusion on their meanings. Culture is a pattern of behavior shared by a society or group of people. Many different things make up a people's culture. These things include food, language, clothing, tools, music, arts, customs, beliefs, and religion.

The term *ethnicity* describes the cultural background of a person. An ethnic group is made up of people who share the same ethnicity. For example, people who are of Spanish descent tend to identify their ethnicity as Hispanic.

Discover! SOCIAL STUDIES • GRADE 3 • LESSON 53

PRACTICE

News Report

Investigate a dispute that might be happening in your community, state, or country. Is a new park or building being developed that people are for or against? Is there a change taking place that is causing people to argue? To find out more about it you can read articles or watch the news to gather information. Maybe you can interview people on each side of the dispute. Then, write a news report about the dispute.

Think about what you've learned about in this chapter. Circle how you feel:

4 – I know this chapter really well. I could teach it to someone.

3 – I know this chapter pretty well.

2 – I am still learning this chapter. I am not sure about some things.

1 – I am confused. I have a lot of questions about what I've learned.

Talk to your instructor about your answers. When you're ready, ask your instructor for the Show What You Know activity for the chapter.

Chapter 11
Scarcity and Choices

Hi there! This is Julia, the grasshopper live and in-person from New York.

Last time, we arrived at the United Nations building. We were ready to tell the world why Mexico and the United States should trade corn and wheat.

Let's hop to it!

My cousin Juan went to the stage. He said, "In my village, we can only grow corn. When it doesn't grow, we have nothing to eat. In places where the corn does grow, we get bored eating the same thing every night!" Everyone in the United Nations building laughed. No one likes to eat the same thing every day!

I also gave a talk. I told the people that in the United States, we have a lot of types of food, but we don't grow everything here. We also need variety, but that is less important. What really matters is that we can help others. "You heard my cousin. When we trade food with other countries, we help them eat better. We also stop them from eating the same boring dinner every night!"

After our speech, we met with the presidents of Mexico and the United States. They both liked our speeches.

I was glad such important people would listen to grasshoppers like us. We made some good points!

Like I always say, good things come to those who hustle!

What Will I Learn?

This chapter looks at resources and their availability. It focuses on how our choices determine the availability of resources.

Lessons at a Glance

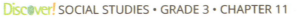

Lesson 54

Resources and Scarcity

By the end of this lesson, you will be able to:

- define the term *scarcity*
- identify examples of resources, wants, and needs

Lesson Review

If you need to review working together, please go to the lesson titled "Cooperation Among Groups and Organizations."

Academic Vocabulary

Read the following vocabulary words and definitions. Look through the lesson. Can you find each vocabulary word? Underline the vocabulary word in your lesson. Write the page number of where you found each word in the blanks.

- **economy:** the wealth and resources of a country or nation (page ____)
- **need:** something we must have to live (page ____)
- **scarcity:** there is a limit to the resources and goods that can be produced (page ____)
- **supply chain:** the process in which goods get from production to buyer (page ____)
- **want:** something we would like to have, but isn't necessary to live (page ____)

Shortage

You may remember in the recent past that there have been shortages of some items that people want and need. There have been shortages on things like toilet paper, yeast, flour, and lumber.

Look for news articles online or through your library that talk about one of these shortages. How did it affect people? What was done about the problem?

Next, imagine that you are a decision maker who can impact the shortage in some way. What can you do to help people access what they need?

Have you ever had a craving for a particular food? A craving is when you really, really want something. You want it so bad you can taste it in your mind and you can't stop thinking about it.

You may have imagined a hot, steaming, gooey slice of pizza.

Maybe you have dreamt of a bite of fluffy cake covered in real buttercream frosting—the kind that the surface almost crackles a bit when you cut a bite with your fork because it is set up so perfectly.

It can be hard to deal with cravings! Are the examples above things that you need or things that you want?

....

....

....

....

You do not truly need pizza or cake to survive. Even though cravings can feel very strong, they're generally just very strong wants.

TAKE A CLOSER LOOK

Have you ever experienced a shortage that affected you? Maybe you really needed a specific thing to finish a project, but the store was all out. Maybe you were looking for a new book, but it was sold out everywhere. Have you ever wanted or needed something you could not get?

What was that experience like? What did you do about it? Discuss your experience with your instructor.

What Is Scarcity?

An **economy** is the wealth and resources of a country or region. Countries, states, cities, and towns all have economies. People work to make products and services that other people buy and use. Each time people spend money, they are participating in the economy.

Scarcity in economics means that there is a limit to the resources and goods that can be produced, and sometimes the demand for these goods will be greater than the supply of the goods available to buy.

For example, if there are four friends who want cookies for a snack, but there are only three cookies, then there aren't enough cookies for all the friends. This is an example of scarcity. There is a scarcity of cookies because there aren't enough cookies for all the friends who want cookies.

A **want** is something we would like to have but don't need to live. A **need** is something we must have to live. Some examples of wants include jewelry, cake, and gaming systems. Some things we need include food, water, air, and shelter.

IN THE REAL WORLD

Problem Solving

Think about the cookie example. There are four friends, but only three cookies. What are two possible solutions to this problem? Share your ideas with your instructor.

WRITE Think about the last time you were at the grocery store. List 10 different items you saw around the store. Circle the items that are needs and underline the items that are wants.

1. ....

2. ....

3. ....

4. ....

5. ....

6. ....

7. ....

8. ....

9. ....

10. ....

READ

Scarcity of Resources

Everything you can find in a store has been on a journey to get to you. We call that journey a **supply chain**. Think about potatoes and potato chips.

A farmer in Idaho grows potatoes. The farmer picks, sorts, and bags the potatoes and then sells them to a company called a supplier who ships the potatoes to your local store. This is a short supply chain—farmer to supplier to store to you!

Now think about potato chips. The farmer picks, sorts and bags potatoes and sells them to a supplier. The supplier sells the potatoes to a company that makes potato chips. The potato chip company peels, slices, cooks, and bags the potato chips. This is called manufacturing because it's done in a factory. The potato chip maker wants to sell a lot of potato chips, so they sell their chips to a distributor who can sell to a lot of different stores—gas stations, grocery stores, and restaurants to name a few. This supply chain is longer—farmer to supplier to manufacturer to distributor to store to you.

If a product is more complicated to make or build, the supply chain is more complicated. Think about a house. You need raw materials like wood to make the lumber. You need manufactured things like air conditioners and water pipes. Then you need special workers like electricians and plumbers. Think of all the supply chains that have to work to make a house.

ONLINE CONNECTION

With the help of an adult, research the container ship the *Ever Given* to see how it made waves in the news—but not in the Suez Canal!

After you finish your research, write a paragraph explaining how this event had an impact on the world's supply chain.

WRITE

Think of two examples of things that could potentially stop the supply chain.

....

....

....

Making Choices

Whenever there is scarcity, choices must be made. What can I do without? Is there an alternative I can use instead? Can I get what I need from another source? It is important to determine what you actually need and what you simply want when there are shortages.

Sometimes you can find what you need by shopping around. You can also talk to your friends and neighbors about working together to access basic necessities if there is a shortage. Some things you can learn to produce yourself, like clothing or food. You can plant a garden or learn to bake bread. Sometimes, though, the only thing to do is wait. Most people can't make their own microchips, so if they need something that relies on microchips, like a new car, they will either need to wait until the new car they want is available, or purchase a used car.

When there are shortages, it can cause the price of goods to increase. When demand is higher than supply, goods become more valuable. With the car example, if there are not many new cars available to purchase, that puts used cars in much higher demand. More people want to buy cars than there are cars available. That makes the price of the cars increase because the cars are more valuable.

If there are more people wanting to buy houses than there are houses on the market, how do you think that will affect the house prices? Explain your answer.

....

....

....

In this lesson, you learned:

- Scarcity means there is a shortage of a particular resource available to buyers.
- Things we want are things we would like to have but are not necessary to live.
- Things we need are things we must have to live.
- Scarcity can be caused by disruptions in the supply chain.
- When there are shortages, buyers have to make choices.

Think About It

How can having a good understanding of the difference between wants and needs help you handle a big shortage?

Discover! SOCIAL STUDIES • GRADE 3 • LESSON 54

1. Define *scarcity*.

....

2. List three ways disruptions in the supply chain can lead to scarcity.

....

....

....

3. Complete the following t-chart by listing five wants in the "Wants" column, and five needs in the "Needs" column.

WANTS	NEEDS

CRE▲TE

It's a great idea to learn how to make things you need or use a lot. Brainstorm things you use often or purchase regularly and make a list. From that list, is there anything you could learn to make yourself?

Research instructions and tips for making that thing. Maybe you'd like to learn how to sew a garment. If you learned to weave tote bags out of scrap fabric or old t-shirts, you wouldn't need grocery bags! Maybe you would like to learn how to bake bread. Maybe you would like to grow your own tomatoes. You could even learn to make a wooden box!

Find out what you would need to get started and work with an adult to complete your project.

Lesson 55

Types of Resources

By the end of this lesson, you will be able to:

- identify and compare examples of natural, human, and capital resources

Lesson Review

If you need to review resources, please go to the lesson titled "Resources and Scarcity."

Academic Vocabulary

Read the following vocabulary words and definitions. Look through the lesson. Can you find each vocabulary word? Underline the vocabulary word in your lesson. Write the page number of where you found each word in the blanks.

- **capital resources:** tools, items, buildings, or goods required to provide goods and services (page ____)
- **goods:** items that people use or sell (page ____)
- **human resources:** people who work to provide a good or a service (page ____)
- **natural resources:** materials found in nature and that are used by people (page ____)
- **resource:** something used for a purpose (page ____)
- **scarcity:** a limit to the resources and goods that can be produced (page ____)
- **services:** activities done to satisfy a want or need (page ____)

IN THE REAL WORLD

Next time you are at the grocery store, take a closer look around you. Everything that you see is a resource from somewhere in our world. Fruit in the produce section was grown, harvested, cleaned, boxed, shipped, unboxed, and put on the shelf. Lots of natural, human, and capital resources go into the food you eat every day!

Ramon's family ordered a pizza for dinner. Ramon's mom and dad each got one slice. Ramon's two older brothers each got a slice. When Ramon and his best friend Sam went to grab their pizza, there was only one slice left! There was not enough pizza for everyone to each have a slice.

If you have ever been in a situation like this, you have experienced scarcity. **Scarcity** is when the amount of a resource cannot keep up with the amount of people that need or want that resource. More people need the resource than the amount of resource available. In Ramon's situation, more people wanted pizza than the number of slices. There was not enough pizza available for everyone.

How should Ramon's family have cut their pizza so there were enough slices for everyone? Divide the pizza below into enough slices for the parents, the three brothers, and Ramon's friend Sam.

Abundance

What is the opposite of scarcity? Abundance is when there is plenty of a resource to go around. Ramon wishes his family had an abundance of pizza! Think of something abundant in your life, something that you have plenty of. Maybe you have an abundance of healthy food, an abundance of love, or an abundance of laughter in your home. Write about something abundant in your life, your community, or your country that you are grateful for.

....
....
....
....
....
....
....
....
....
....

Scarcity can cause problems when we do not have enough of the things that we need. What happens when people experience scarcity with things they need? Let's learn about scarcity and some examples of resources, needs, and wants.

Needs and Wants

Needs are things that are necessary for survival such as food, water, shelter, and love. *Wants* are things that you would like to have but are not necessary for survival. Many people have different things that they want and need. For example, some families in rural areas need a car to get to work or the grocery store. Families who live in cities may be able to take a train or a bus, so having a car is not necessary for them.

People who live in different regions also have different wants and needs. People who live in cold climates need heavy coats and clothing to protect their bodies from low temperatures. People who live in hot climates need light layers and breathable clothing to keep their bodies cool.

These are both pictures of homes. Shelter in the form of a home is necessary for human survival. Some people have big homes, and some people have small homes. Apartments are homes, and some people live in mobile homes or RVs. There are many types of homes! All homes are wonderful homes if they are safe places to live and sleep.

Goods and Services

The things that we need or want can be either goods or services. **Goods** are material items that people can purchase. **Services** are activities done to satisfy a want or need. Look at the chart below to see some examples of goods and services.

Goods	Services
toys	washing dishes
games	cutting hair
crayons	teaching kids
cars	serving food
food	driving a truck
cell phones	delivering mail
school supplies	collecting trash

READ

Resources

A **resource** is something used for a purpose. Three different types of resources are **natural resources**, **human resources**, and **capital resources**.

Type of Resource	Definition	Examples	Importance
natural resources	materials found in nature used by people	water, soil, wood, coal	can be used to make almost everything we need
human resources	people who work to provide a good or a service	teacher, librarian, waitress, painter	people in our communities who do important jobs and help others
capital resources	the tools, items, buildings, or goods required to provide goods and services	dump truck, lawnmower, factory, hammer	allow humans to make the goods and services we need and want

WRITE

Why are human, natural, and capital resources all important?

....

....

....

....

....

....

IN THE REAL WORLD

Imagine you were to set up a lemonade stand in your neighborhood. Think about the goods being purchased and services being provided. Think of all the natural, capital, and human resources that would be necessary to make the stand successful.

Write a list of all the resources that you would need to operate your lemonade stand.

....

....

....

PRACTICE

Write *natural*, *human*, or *capital* to describe the resources below.

1. _____

2. _____

3. _____

4. _____

5. _____

6. _____

READ

Scarcity

Some resources are plentiful, whereas others are more scarce. The availability of resources varies from place to place.

In Southern California, sunshine is plentiful while water is scarce. Many people have solar panels to harvest the sun's rays and convert them into energy. This is a natural resource that people in Southern California have plenty of because it only rains a few days each year. However, all those sunny days lead to a lack of water. The ground is hard and dry. Rivers and lakes have dried up. Since Southern California gets such little rainfall, the demand for water is much greater than the supply. This makes water a scarcity. Because water is a scarcity, Californians have to pay more money for the water in their homes.

Many times, a shortage of resources causes the price of the resource to increase, just like the water in California. This is called supply and demand. If there is a large supply of a resource and only a small demand for it, the cost decreases. If there is a small supply of a resource and a large demand, the cost increases.

We see supply and demand change the price of gasoline regularly. When more drilling occurs, there is a greater supply of gasoline. Gas stations do not have to charge as much money per gallon of gas. When there is less of a supply, the cost of gas goes up.

WRITE Describe something that experiences scarcity and what makes it scarce.

....
....
....

REVIEW

In this lesson, you learned:

- Scarcity is when the supply of a resource cannot meet the demand for that resource.
- There are natural resources, human resources, and capital resources, all of which are important to providing goods and services to people.
- Needs are things that are necessary for survival such as food, water, and shelter.
- Wants are things that you would like to have but are not necessary for survival.

Think About It
What resources are you using right now? Can you find an example of a natural resource, a human resource, and a capital resource in the room you are in?

Write the word *need* or *want* to describe the pictures below.

1. _____

2. _____

3. _____

4. _____

5. _____

6. _____

7. _____

8. _____

Circle the correct answer.

9. What is an example of scarcity?

   A. There are too many tomatoes growing in Stacy's garden, so she gives some away.

   B. People need to purchase food from grocery stores in order to survive.

   C. Overfishing caused a shortage of tuna populations in the ocean, and now grocery chains are having a hard time supplying their stores.

   D. Concerts are sold out when all of the tickets have been purchased.

10. Which best describes a natural resource?

    A. materials found in nature and that are used by people

    B. people who work to provide a good or a service

    C. tools, items, buildings, or goods required to provide goods and services

    D. something used for a purpose

11. Which of these is NOT an example of a need?

    A. healthy food

    B. a family

    C. new headphones

    D. a vehicle to get to school and work

12. Toys, games, food, school supplies, and cars—what are these all examples of?

    A. services   C. needs

    B. goods   D. wants

CREATE

Create a collage with examples of needs, wants, goods, and services. Fold a piece of construction paper into fourths. Label one section *needs*, one section *wants*, one section *goods*, and the last section *services*. Ask your instructor for an old magazine. Look in the magazine for examples of each category. Cut out the images and glue them onto your collage. Share your creation with your instructor or your family members.

13. What is an example of a capital resource?

    A. A nutritionist creates a plan for someone to eat healthier meals.

    B. A doctor gives a checkup.

    C. A construction worker needs a hammer to help them build a house.

    D. A fish uses its gills to breathe underwater.

14. What is an example of a human resource?

    A. a grocery store   C. a good or service

    B. a librarian   D. a factory

Lesson 56

Natural Resources

By the end of this lesson, you will be able to:

- identify important natural resources
- classify natural resources as renewable or nonrenewable

Lesson Review

If you need to review what resources are, please go to the lesson titled "Resources and Scarcity."

Academic Vocabulary

Read the following vocabulary words and definitions. Look through the lesson. Can you find each vocabulary word? Underline the vocabulary word in your lesson. Write the page number of where you found each word in the blanks.

- **deforestation:** the clearing or cutting down of forests (page ___)
- **natural resources:** materials found in nature and that are used by people (page ___)
- **non-renewable resources:** environmental resources that we use faster than we can make, clean, or regrow (page ___)
- **recycling:** the process of taking materials ready to be thrown away and turning them into reusable materials (page ___)
- **renewable resources:** natural resources that can be cleaned or regrown quickly so that we never run out (page ___)

PLAY

The sun is an important natural resource! Can you imagine a world without sunlight? If the sun were to suddenly disappear, we would not notice on Earth right away. Nine minutes later, though, we would find ourselves in complete darkness. What would this be like?

At night once the sun goes down, turn off all the lights and close all the curtains. It should get pretty dark! Then try to complete an activity in the complete darkness like brushing your teeth or tying your shoes. Can you do it without any light?

Did you know recycling can help protect our natural resources? When we **recycle**, we take materials ready to be thrown away and turn them into reusable materials. We can make new materials out of recyclables so we don't have to use more natural resources. For example, recycling can protect trees, one of Earth's natural resources. Cardboard is made from harvested trees, but cardboard can also be made from recycled paper products. When we recycle paper products, we are protecting trees from being cut down and harvested.

Recycling is a wonderful way to help conserve our planet's natural resources. Many towns have recycling bins similar to trash cans. Some towns have recycling centers where people drop off their recycling. Unfortunately, not

all towns have recycling programs. As you complete this lesson, think about the different things you could do to help protect our natural resources.

What are some things that your family recycles? List six things your family recycles.

....

....

....

TAKE A CLOSER LOOK

For one day, collect a bag of your family's trash. Ask your instructor for a pair of rubber gloves and lay some newspaper out on the floor or on the ground outside. Carefully dump out the bag of trash so that all the trash goes on the newspaper. Look closely: Can anything in the trash be recycled? Many times, recycling is accidentally thrown into the trash can! Discuss your findings with your instructor.

What Is a Natural Resource?

Natural resources are materials found in nature that are used by people. Some natural resources are necessary for life, whereas others have economic value and contribute to industry. Some of Earth's most familiar natural resources include air, water, soil, wildlife, forests, minerals, and fossil fuels. All living things depend on natural resources to survive. People need water to drink, air to breathe, and wood or metal to build shelter. We also need fuel to power our cars and heat our homes.

Air is the most important natural resource because all living things need air to breathe. It's a good thing we have plenty of air in Earth's atmosphere! Pollution makes our air dirty and bad to breathe. It is important to limit the amount of pollution so that we have enough clean air to breathe.

Water is another one of the most important natural resources. Every living thing needs water to survive. Water can be found in oceans, rivers, lakes, underground, and frozen in glaciers. Only a small amount of water on Earth is fresh water, which can be used to drink. It is important to keep fresh water clean and to limit the amount of fresh water that we use so that everyone has enough.

Natural resources are not evenly distributed around Earth. For example, some areas have plenty of water, while other places may get very little rainfall so water is scarce. Countries that have lots of natural resources can sell their resources to other countries. For example, countries with large forests generally sell lots of wood, paper, and paper products.

READ

Renewable and Nonrenewable Resources

There are two types of natural resources: renewable resources and non-renewable resources. **Renewable resources** can be cleaned or regrown quickly so that we never run out. Some renewable resources are only renewable if they are replaced, such as trees. When trees are chopped down to make lumber and paper products, new trees can be planted to replace them.

Non-renewable resources are natural resources that cannot be replaced after they are used. One example of a nonrenewable resource is fossil fuels. Fossil fuels were formed from the buried remains of ancient plants and animals over many years. Petroleum is a fossil fuel that is used to make oil and gasoline.

RENEWABLE RESOURCES	NONRENEWABLE RESOURCES
▪ air	
▪ water	▪ rock
▪ soil	▪ minerals
▪ plants	▪ metals
▪ animals	▪ uranium
▪ wind	▪ fossil fuels, like petroleum, coal, and
▪ the sun	natural gas

WRITE

Why is it important to replace some renewable resources?

....

....

....

IN THE REAL WORLD

Deforestation is what happens when an entire forest of trees is harvested at one time. This causes lots of environmental problems, such as:

- less oxygen in the atmosphere
- more carbon dioxide in the atmosphere from trees being burned
- erosion
- habitat loss for animals

The largest amount of deforestation is happening in tropical areas, where rainforests are being cut down. Most deforestation is permanent. Some areas do recover from this damage, but it can take many years.

Making Energy With Renewable Resources

New ways of using renewable resources have been developed to protect natural resources. Scientists and experts create ways to use renewable resources for things like electricity. The sun is a renewable resource becoming more efficient to use. The sun has been a natural resource for years! The sun has been used to heat food, keep people warm, and dry clothes. Researchers learned that the sun's rays could be transformed into energy using solar panels. Today solar panels are installed on the roofs of homes, on buildings, over parking lots, and even on "solar farms" where lots of solar panels are installed in big fields! If you see big shiny panels on the roof of a house, that house is using solar energy. Solar energy can power anything in your house that needs electricity.

Another renewable energy source is wind. Wind turbines are large propeller-like blades that generate power through wind. Wind spins the blades around a rotor, which spins a generator, which creates electricity. It works just like a pinwheel!

With more renewable energy sources, more people are switching to electric vehicles. Electric vehicles are cars that are powered by electricity. Electric vehicles are better for the environment because they use renewable energy instead of non-renewable gasoline.

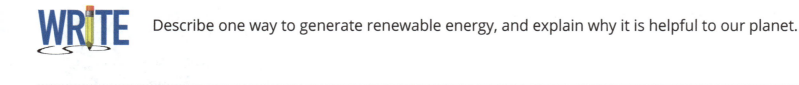

WRITE

Describe one way to generate renewable energy, and explain why it is helpful to our planet.

....

....

....

....

PRACTICE

Look around your home for examples of natural resources. What can you find? Draw pictures of some things made with natural resources in the box below and label the natural resource used.

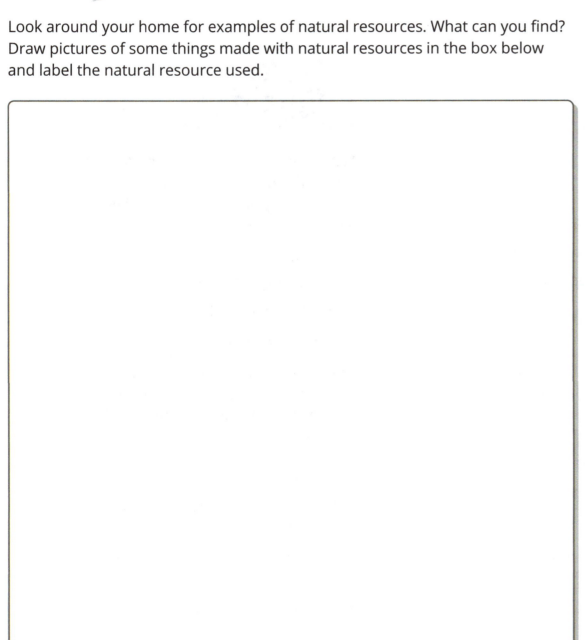

REVIEW

In this lesson, you learned:

- Natural resources are materials found in nature that are used by people.

- Some natural resources are renewable and will never run out, while other resources are nonrenewable, and we will eventually run out of them.

- It is important to protect both renewable and non-renewable natural resources.

- Recycling and using new ways of generating energy can help protect our natural resources.

Think About It
What can you do to help protect Earth's natural resources?

SHOW WHAT YOU KNOW

Circle the correct answer.

1. What are natural resources?

   A. things that protect plants and animals

   B. materials found in nature that are used by people

   C. materials used by animals to build their habitats

   D. things that are made by humans

2. Which one of these is an example of a natural resource?

   A. plastic

   B. a computer

   C. petroleum gasoline

   D. a stuffed animal

3. Resources that can be cleaned or regrown quickly so that we never run out are called _____.

   A. renewable resources

   B. non-renewable resources

   C. human resources

   D. capital resources

4. Which is an example of a nonrenewable resource?

   A. water

   B. sunlight

   C. animals

   D. minerals

5. What is deforestation?

   A. when an entire forest of trees is harvested at one time

   B. when a bunch of trees are planted at once to make a forest

   C. when a forest is cleaned to eliminate diseases

   D. when one tree is cut down

ONLINE CONNECTION

With your instructor, research a few ways to reduce the amount of natural resources you are using in your home. Here are keywords to search for:

- reducing waste
- creating a greener home
- recycling tips for kids
- conservation of natural resources

Then share with your family some tips for conserving electricity, using less water, or recycling. The planet will thank you!

6. What are solar panels used for?

   A. to protect houses from the sun's powerful rays

   B. to harvest energy from the wind

   C. to harvest energy from the sun's rays

   D. to charge electric vehicles

7. Explain two ways that you can help to protect natural resources.

....

....

....

....

....

....

....

....

....

....

Lesson 57

Making Choices

By the end of this lesson, you will be able to:

- explain what is given up when making a choice
- identify reasons people make a choice
- describe how buyers make choices about their wants and needs through purchases
- identify types of advertising designed to influence personal choice

Lesson Review

If you need to review wants and needs, please go to the lesson titled "Resources and Scarcity."

Academic Vocabulary

Read the following vocabulary words and definitions. Look through the lesson. Can you find each vocabulary word? Underline the vocabulary word in your lesson. Write the page number of where you found each word in the blanks.

- **advertisement:** a notice or announcement of a product or service to persuade people to buy things (page ____)
- **choice:** the act of picking between two or more possibilities (page ____)
- **opportunity cost:** benefits or returns you miss out on when choosing one alternative over another (page ____)

ONLINE CONNECTION

Using an online search engine, investigate three different advertisements. These advertisements can be shown as a poster image, audio file, or commercial. Study the features of these advertisements, such as the color used and the size and font of the text. If you obtain an audio file, listen to the host's voice or the sound and volume of the music in the background. Then, rank these advertisements from most favorite to least favorite. Explain how you ranked these advertisements on a separate piece of paper. Share your results with your instructor.

Did you know that people can make thousands of choices each day? A **choice** is the act of picking between two or more possibilities. People make choices, such as what to eat, what to wear, how much money to spend, what to say, or what to do. These choices can be used to satisfy people's wants and needs.

However, the line between wants and needs can sometimes be blurred. This can happen when you see an advertisement that draws your attention. For example, imagine you are on a trip to buy school supplies. At the store, you see a store clerk showing people a new backpack that is remote controlled! You may convince yourself that you *want* the backpack because it looks flattering and *need* it for the convenience. Ads are used to persuade people to buy things!

Take a look at these images that show different types of advertisements. What makes them capture people's attention? Write your ideas in the lines below.

....

....

....

....

....

....

hamburger ad

bubble tea ad

Father's Day sale ad

Making Choices

In the Explore section, you learned that people make choices to satisfy their wants and needs. For example, suppose a parent gave you $5 to buy a snack from the store. You see that your favorite snack costs $2, but if you buy two snacks, it costs $3.50. This means you'd be saving money if you buy more! What would you do in this situation to make a good choice? Making good choices are important because they can have an impact on your life! Good choices require time to think things through. Time helps people to decide if a choice is healthy, kind, and safe. For example, is it healthy to eat two snacks? If I buy two snacks, could I show kindness by sharing them with my family and friends? Would it be safer for me to buy only one snack so I can save the money for something else? You may be tempted to buy two snacks at a time because you *want* them. However, buyers make good choices based on how much they *need* something.

When people make choices, they give up the value of the next best thing. The benefits or returns you miss out on when choosing one alternative over another are called **opportunity costs**. If you choose to eat ice cream over fruits, you give up eating something healthier, which may make you feel sick.

choosing a snack to buy

How can people make good choices before they buy something?

....

....

....

....

....

Discover! SOCIAL STUDIES • GRADE 3 • LESSON 57

READ

Advertisements

Have you ever visited a website and noticed the advertisements that pop up? **Advertisements**, also known as ads, are notices or announcements of a product or service that persuade people to buy things. There are many types of ads, such as digital, print, outdoor, and audio. You can find digital ads when you browse the internet, watch TV, or use social media. If you've ever flipped through a magazine, you may have noticed coupons for food and clothing. Ads that are shown in printed form, such as flyers, brochures, or magazines are known as print ads. Outdoor ads are those that can be seen on posters or billboards. You can also hear ads on radios, known as audio ads. The diversity of ads is designed to reach as many people as possible.

ads in Times Square

The main goal of ads is to influence people to buy a product or service. People can be drawn to ads by seeing bright colors or large words. For example, stores may promote sales by displaying vibrant colors of orange and red in their ads. They may also write discounts in large letters in their ads! Some ads may even target specific age groups to influence people to buy their products. For example, a fast food restaurant may offer a special toy for every kids' meal that is bought.

WRITE

How do different types of advertisements influence people to buy a product or service?

....
....
....
....
....

PRACTICE

Using what you know about making choices and the types of advertisements, create an ad for each of the following situations.

SCENARIOS	AD DRAWING
Selling Cookies	
Selling Clothes	
Selling Tickets to a Show	

REVIEW

In this lesson, you learned:

- Making good choices is important because they can have an impact on your life.

- Good choices require time to think things through. Time helps people to decide if a choice is healthy, kind, and safe.

- Buyers make good choices based on how much they need rather than want something.

- When people make choices, they give up the value of the next best thing. This is called the opportunity cost.

- There are many types of ads, such as digital, print, outdoor, and audio.

- The main goal of ads is to influence people to buy a product or service.

- People can be influenced by ads when they see bright colors or large words.

Think About It

How can advertisements be misleading or dishonest?

SHOW WHAT YOU KNOW

Circle the correct answer for each question.

1. When people make choices, they give up the value of the next best thing. This is called _____.

   A. an advertisement

   B. the opportunity cost

   C. satisfying wants and needs

2. Before people make the choice to buy something, what should they consider? Circle all correct answers.

   A. if the choice is healthy

   B. if the choice is safe

   C. if the choice saves time

Fill in the missing word to complete the sentences.

3. The main goal of advertisements is to influence people to _____ a product or service.

4. Types of advertisements include digital, _____, outdoor, and audio.

5. How do buyers make choices about their wants and needs through purchases? You can use examples from your life.

   ....

   ....

   ....

   ....

TAKE A CLOSER LOOK

Did you know that many restaurants and stores offer reward programs? These rewards are given to customers who make a purchase. For example, a customer could earn two points for every dollar they spend. When they reach a certain number of points, they can get rewards. Reward programs encourage people to buy more so they can save more! Do you think more stores should do this? Why or why not? Share your answers with an instructor.

6. Suppose you are having a bake sale to raise money for a new school playground. To spread the word, your teacher asks you to make two different types of advertisements. What advertisements would you make? What would you include in your advertisements to attract people's attention to them?

   ....

   ....

   ....

   ....

Chapter 11 Review

In this lesson, you will:

- review the information from the lessons in Chapter 11, "Scarcity and Choices."

Lesson Review

Throughout the chapter, we have learned the following big ideas:

- In economics, scarcity is defined as a limit to the resources and goods that can be produced. Resources that people would like to have but do not need to live is a want. By contrast, a need is something people must have to survive. (Lesson 54)
- Natural resources, human resources, and capital resources are important to providing goods and services to people. (Lesson 55)
- Renewable resources are natural resources that can be cleaned or regrown quickly so that people never run out. Non-renewable resources are natural resources that cannot be replaced after they are used. (Lesson 56)
- When people make choices, they give up the value of the next best thing. This is called the opportunity cost. (Lesson 57)

Go back and review the lessons as needed while you complete the activities.

CREATE

Imagine you are designing a business or service where people can purchase goods. This could be a toy store, ice cream stand, or bookstore. Make a list of goods you would sell. Include the price for each item. Design a poster or flyer advertising your business. Include your store's name. Explain how your business will benefit your customers.

Economy and Scarcity

You learned about the economy and scarcity of resources. An economy is the wealth and resources of a country or region. The study of the economy is called economics. People work to make products and services that people buy and use. People participate in the economy each time they spend money to buy goods and services. Companies participate in the economy each time they produce services or buy goods and services.

In economics, scarcity refers to the limit of the resources and goods that can be produced. Sometimes, the demand for goods will be greater than the supply of goods available to buy. For example, imagine 100 people want to buy tickets for a concert but only 50 tickets are available. This is a scarcity of tickets because there are not enough tickets for 100 people to buy.

You also learned that the availability of resources in a supply chain is needed to make and sell products. A supply chain is the process of moving goods and services from the supplier to customer. Every item you find in a store has been in a supply chain on its way to you. Think about your favorite potato chips. Before potato chips are sold in a store, a farmer picks, sorts, and bags the potatoes. Follow the arrows below to see what happens next.

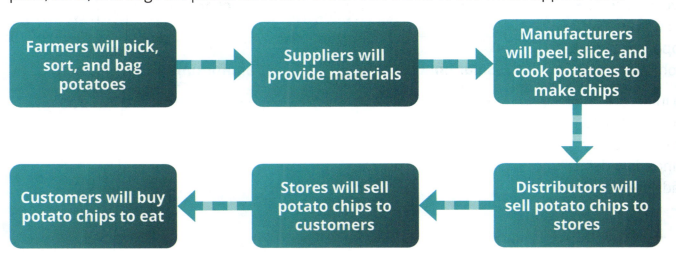

TAKE A CLOSER LOOK

Goods and Services

The things that we need or want are either goods or services. Goods are material items that people can purchase. Services are activities done to satisfy a want or need. Look at the chart below to see some examples of goods and services.

Goods	Services
toys	washing dishes
games	cutting hair
crayons	teaching students
cars	
food	serving food
cell phones	driving a truck
school supplies	delivering mail
	collecting trash

REVIEW

Resources and Making Choices

Natural resources are materials found in nature that people use. The two types of natural resources are renewable resources and non-renewable resources. Renewable resources are natural resources that can be cleaned or regrown quickly. Examples of renewable resources are oxygen, water, timber, and solar energy. Non-renewable resources are natural resources that cannot be replaced after they are used. Earth has only a fixed amount of these resources. Examples of non-renewable resources are fossil fuels, such as natural gas and coal, metals, such as aluminum, and minerals, such as iron, are also non-renewable.

Buyers make good choices by purchasing items based on how much they need something rather than how much they want something. A need is something people must have, such as food to eat or a shelter to live in. A want is something people do not need to survive, such as jewelry. When people make choices, there is an opportunity cost. This means they may not be able to buy something else.

Companies use advertisements, or ads, to influence people to buy something. Ads are announcements of a product or service designed to persuade people to buy things. Ads can be found online, in magazines, in videos, on the radio, or outdoors. Many types of ads are used to reach as many people as possible.

Resources

Have you ever wondered how natural resources are used? The table below shows how some common renewable and non-renewable resources are used in everyday life.

Renewable	How They Are Used	Non-renewable	How They Are Used
timber	• make paper • build houses	natural gas	• light a fire • heat water
cotton	• make clothing	coal	• generate electricity
solar energy	• generate electricity	aluminum	• make cans and kitchen utensils

PRACTICE

Vocabulary Graphic Organizer

Read each vocabulary word shown below. Then, fill in the graphic organizer.

Word	Definition	Use the word in a sentence
scarcity		
want		
need		
economy		
natural resources		
advertisement		

PRACTICE

Renewable and Non-renewable Resources

Using what you know about natural resources, determine if each image represents a renewable or a nonrenewable resource.

....
....
....

....
....
....

....
....
....

....
....
....

....
....
....

....
....
....

Discover! SOCIAL STUDIES • GRADE 3 • LESSON 58

PRACTICE

Goods and Services Venn Diagram

Using what you know about goods and services, fill in the Venn diagram below. You may refer to the worktext or use examples from your daily life to complete this diagram.

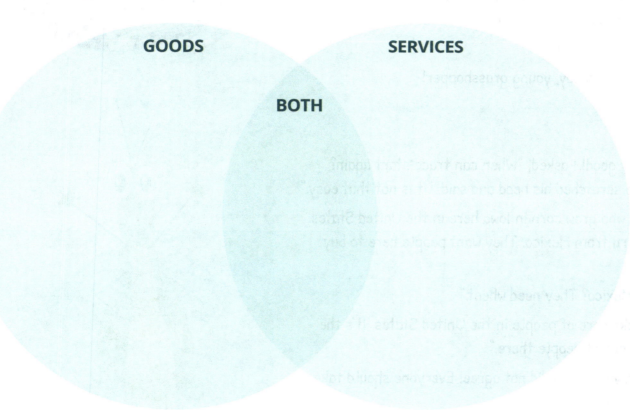

GOODS

SERVICES

BOTH

Economic Systems

Hi, my friend. Remember me? It is Julia, the grasshopper!

My cousin Juan and I spoke at the United Nations. All of the leaders of the world heard us talk. We explained why trade between countries is so important.

After we talked, I met the president! I was so excited.

Do you want to hear what he told me? Then, be ready, young grasshopper!

The president said my speech was very good! I asked, "When can trade start again?" The president looked embarrassed. He scratched his head and said, "It is not that easy."

The president said, "We have farmers who grow corn in Iowa here in the United States. They think we should not be buying corn from Mexico. They want people here to buy from farmers in the United States."

I asked, "Shouldn't we help people in Mexico? They need wheat."

The president nodded. "My job is to take care of people in the United States. It's the job of the Mexican president to take care of people there."

I understood what the president was saying. But I did not agree! Everyone should take care of one another, no matter where they are born.

I had to do something to convince him. But I did not know what. Do you think I could change his mind? I was ready to hustle!

Like I always say, good things come to those who hustle!

What Will I Learn?

This chapter examines how economies operate on the national level. It looks at how local economies and businesses fit into national economic systems of goods and services.

Lessons at a Glance

self-service

Lesson 59

Goods and Services

By the end of this lesson, you will be able to:

- identify goods, services, consumers, and producers in the local community
- identify competing sellers in the local market

Lesson Review

If you need to review economic choices, please go to the lesson titled "Making Choices."

Academic Vocabulary

Read the following vocabulary words and definitions. Look through the lesson. Can you find each vocabulary word? Underline the vocabulary word in your lesson. Write the page number of where you found each word in the blanks.

- **business:** an organization that offers goods and services for sale (page ___)
- **competition:** when more than one producer offers the same goods or services (page ___)
- **consumers:** people who buy goods and services (page ___)
- **goods:** items that people use or sell (page ___)
- **producers:** people who makes goods or offers services (page ___)
- **services:** activities done to satisfy a want or need (page ___)

IN THE REAL WORLD

Before someone can open a new business, they need to make a business plan. A business plan helps business owners stay focused on their purpose and goals. It can also be used to get loans from a bank or money from investors.

If you were to open a store or restaurant in your community one day, what kind of business would it be? Make a plan for your business by completing the table below. Use separate paper if needed.

What will your business be?	
Why does your community need it?	
Who else has a similar business in your community?	
How will your business be different from other similar businesses?	

Look at this picture:

Have you ever been to a market like this? This is a farmers market. This is a type of market where local farmers can sell the food and other goods they produce. Some farmers also grow flowers to sell, and some sell honey from the bees they raise. Other people sell handmade items like soaps and jams.

Where can people buy food in your community? Share your answers with your instructor.

PLAY

Pretend you had $20 to spend on anything you want. There is only one catch: you have to spend it all within seven miles of your house. With the help of an adult, do some online shopping—just make sure the businesses are close to home!

Where would you go? What would you buy? Make a list of items and their prices. Add all the prices to make sure you stay under your $20 budget. Share your list with your instructor.

READ

Different Opinions on Goods and Services

Goods are items that people use or sell. Some goods are things you need like food, clothes, and a place to live. Some goods are things you want like a game system or headphones.

Name two stores where you buy things you need close to your home. Name two stores where you could buy things you want.

....

....

Services

Services are activities done to satisfy a want or need. Teaching is a service. Driving a bus is a service. Cutting hair is a service.

Think of two services you or your family depend on. Ask your instructor for ideas if you cannot think of any services.

....

....

People who buy goods and services are called **consumers**. Businesses and people who make goods and offer services are called **producers**.

Have you ever been a consumer? Write an example of a time you were a consumer. Have you ever been a producer? Write an example of a time when you were a producer.

....

....

....

There are services everywhere you look in communities!

My Community

How far do you have to go to buy food? Do you have to drive? Can you walk there? Different kinds of communities provide you with the goods and services you need and want in different ways. If you live in a really small town, you might have to drive many miles to shop for food or clothes. If you live in a big city, you probably do not have to drive so far. How far do you have to go to find things you need? Discuss this with your instructor.

Services can also be very different in cities and towns. Imagine that your sink gets backed up and you need a plumber to fix it. How many plumbers can you choose from? In a city, there might be 50 plumbers. In a small town, there might be two. If you have choices, how do you decide which one to call? Ask your instructor how they would choose.

When there are many producers offering similar goods and services, they have to compete for your business. Some producers will offer a lower price to get your business but may not be able to afford to give you great service. Some will offer a higher price but provide better service. This is called competition. **Competition** happens when more than one producer offers the same goods or services in the same area. The producer tries to give you a reason to choose them.

ONLINE CONNECTION

With the help of an adult, look up instructions online for opening a lemonade stand. What would it take to become a lemonade producer for a day? Consider the following things:

- What supplies do you need?

- Would you need to buy supplies, and how would you pay for them?

- How much money would you need to make to cover your costs?

- How much would you charge per cup?

- How will you attract customers?

Discuss your responses to these questions with your instructor. If you have permission and the ability to do so safely, set up a lemonade stand. After you close up shop, write a paragraph about what you learned.

PRACTICE

Circle the pictures featuring producers.

1.

2.

3.

4.

5.

6.

WRITE

Now that you know something about goods, services, consumers, and producers, it is time to show what you know. Write down why you like to shop at your favorite store. Make sure you include details about the goods or services you like at that store.

....

....

....

....

Circle the correct answer.

1. True or False   Goods are actions of helping or doing work for someone.

2. True or False   A consumer buys goods or services.

3. True or False   A producer makes goods or provides services.

4. True or False   A mechanic is a consumer.

5. True or False   Competition means you are the only business in your community who sells a good or service.

6. True or False   A toy is an example of a service.

7. True or False   When you buy balloons and someone puts helium in them for you, this is an example of a good and a service.

8. List one example of competing goods you can find in your area and one example of competing services you can find in your area.

A. ....

B. ....

At the beginning of the lesson, you made a business plan. Now it is time to take the next step. Name your business and design a logo to represent your business. Use a separate sheet of paper to plan or try out different names and designs, then put your favorite name and design here to show to your instructor.

Lesson 60

Money and Banks

By the end of this lesson, you will be able to:

- demonstrate the importance of money in everyday life
- identify the role of banks in communities

Lesson Review

If you need to review goods and services, please go to the lesson titled "Goods and Services."

Academic Vocabulary

Read the following vocabulary words and definitions. Look through the lesson. Can you find each vocabulary word? Underline the vocabulary word in your lesson. Write the page number of where you found each word in the blanks.

- **bank:** a business where people deposit, withdraw, and borrow money (page ____)
- **check:** an instruction to the bank to pay out money from that person's account (page ____)
- **deposit:** to put money in a bank account (page ____)
- **interest:** a fee paid for borrowing money (page ____)
- **loan:** money that is borrowed and expected to be paid back with interest (page ____)
- **stock:** a share of ownership in a company (page ____)

ONLINE CONNECTION

Have you ever wanted to buy something but did not have enough money? Perhaps you want a new computer, but you have only $30 in your piggy bank. You can make do without a new computer, save money until you have enough to buy it, or buy the computer on credit by using a credit card. Go online to research what a credit card is and how it works. Then compare a credit card to a debit card. How are they similar or different? Investigate what they look like, how people can get them, and how they are beneficial for banks. Share your answers by creating a slideshow presentation.

Suppose you won $100 for an essay contest in school. How would you spend it? Would you buy yourself new clothes, toys, games, or electronics? Would you consider saving your money to buy something you really want or need in the future? Your parents may have encouraged you not to impulse buy. An impulse buy is when you have a strong desire to buy things that you do not necessarily need, such as toys or the latest gadgets. Your parents may have also asked you to keep your money safe by storing it in a piggy bank or safe.

But how do you keep a large amount of money, such as thousands of dollars, safe? It certainly would not be practical to store that money in a piggy bank. And keeping it in a safe at home might sound good, but money can be lost or stolen. Money can even be destroyed during unexpected events like fires and floods! As a result, many people keep their money safe by storing it in **banks**.

How do you think banks keep people's money safe? Write your ideas in the lines below.

....

....

....

....

TAKE A CLOSER LOOK

Debit cards look almost identical to credit cards. Both cards have a unique 16-digit card number, expiration date, magnetic strip, and EMV chip for security. They also feature the cardholder's full name and the name of the credit card company or bank.

Credit and Debit Cards

READ

Importance of Money

How do people spend the money they earn? People use money to buy essential things like food to eat, a house to live in, clothes to wear, or a doctor visit to get medicine. People can also spend money on nonessential things, or things that people do not necessarily need. These could include buying movie tickets or jewelry.

However, people may also use money to pay off debt. For example, suppose your parents agreed to enroll you in swimming lessons, which are expensive. If your swimming lessons cost $500, your parents may be able to pay for them in small amounts. This is known as paying in installments. Instead of spending $500 at once, your parents can agree to pay $100 per month for five months.

Without money, life can be very hard for people. During the 1920s, many people invested their money in **stocks**. In 1929, these stocks fell, or "crashed," which meant that they were worth nothing. Businesses closed and banks failed, causing people to lose all the money they had! This caused widespread hunger, homelessness, and disease. This event was known as the Great Depression, which lasted 12 years!

Buying Groceries

WRITE

How do people use money in their daily lives?

....

....

....

....

READ

Importance of Banks

Suppose you are on your way to the bank to open up a new bank account. The banker asks if you want to open a savings or checking account. What is the difference? People open a savings account to store money safely and earn **interest**. This means the bank pays you a certain amount of money for every dollar that you store in your savings account. If you **deposit** $100 in your savings account and your interest is one percent, you will earn a dollar every month! How is this possible? The reason for this is because banks make money by lending money to people. If people do not have enough money to buy something big, such as a house or car, they borrow money from the bank. This is called a **loan**. However, banks expect people to pay the money back with interest. This means if you borrow $10 from a bank, you get the money right away. But when you pay back the $10, the bank may charge you interest of a dollar or more. You may end up returning at least eleven dollars to the bank for borrowing money!

A checking account also helps people store money safely. It is mainly used for people who have daily cash needs. For example, if a person buys food from a grocery store and forgets cash, they may write a **check**. People can also use a debit card to pay out money from their checking accounts. Unlike a savings account, checking accounts reward people with little or no interest.

WRITE

What are the differences between a savings and checking account?

....

....

....

....

....

....

Withdrawing Money From a Bank

PRACTICE

Using what you know about the importance of money and banks, complete the table below.

	IMPORTANT FEATURES	HOW PEOPLE USE IN THEIR DAILY LIVES	HOW YOU USE IN YOUR DAILY LIFE
Money			
Banks			

REVIEW

In this lesson, you learned:

- People use money to buy essential things, such as food or houses.

- People also use money on nonessential things, such as movie tickets.

- The Great Depression of 1929 caused stores to close and banks to fail, causing people to lose all their money.

- People open a savings account to store money safely and earn interest.

- A checking account also helps people store money safely. It is mainly used for people who have daily cash needs.

Think About It

What are some of the problems people may encounter when they open a savings or checking account?

Fill in the blank with a word from the Word Bank.

Word Bank: interest   loan   essential

1. Items that are necessary for people to buy, such as food, shelter, and clothing, are called _____ things.

2. _____ is when a bank pays you a certain amount of money for every dollar you store in your savings account.

3. If you do not have enough money to pay for something, you can borrow money from the bank to pay back later. This is called a _____.

Circle all of the correct answers for each question.

4. What are the features of a savings account?

    A. stores and keeps money safe

    B. helps people earn interest

    C. gives people a debit card to access money

5. What are the features of a checking account?

    A. provides checks for people to write and make purchases

    B. charges people interest

    C. stores and keeps money safe

What happens to a person's money if a bank fails? The Federal Deposit Insurance Corporation (FDIC) aims to keep people's money safe in the United States. If money is lost, the FDIC will replace up to $250,000 per person! It also monitors banks for problems or failings. During the Great Depression of 1929, many people lost all their savings in the bank because the FDIC did not exist. Using the internet, research the history of the FDIC. Create a brochure to share your answers.

6. Explain the importance of money in everyday life. Give two examples showing how and why people use money.

....

....

....

....

7. Imagine that a bank lends you $50. What is this called? How can a bank earn money through this process?

....

....

....

....

Lesson 61

Local Economies

By the end of this lesson, you will be able to:

- identify characteristics of a local economy
- describe basic financial needs and how different communities support and sustain themselves

Lesson Review

If you need to review currency, please go to the lesson titled "Money and Banks."

Academic Vocabulary

Read the following vocabulary words and definitions. Look through the lesson. Can you find each vocabulary word? Underline the vocabulary word in your lesson. Write the page number of where you found each word in the blanks.

- **local economy:** the wealth and resources of a community (page ___)
- **public safety:** police, fire, and emergency health services (page ___)
- **public utilities:** water, electrical, and/or gas systems connected to homes and businesses (page ___)
- **skilled labor:** a person with a special job skill (page___)

CREATE

On a piece of paper, draw a community at work. Show how people make money and spend money. Show places where people shop and find entertainment. Show places where people work to make money. Title your picture "Local Economy." Explain your drawing to your instructor.

EXPLRE

What is local? Say you live on a farm or ranch. You might hear your parent say, "I'm going to town. Do you want anything?" That town might be 15 miles away.

Maybe you live in a small town and every August your parent says, "Time for new clothes! We're going to the city!" That city is 40 miles away.

Maybe you live in a suburb or city and you want to see a movie. Your parent says, "The movie is showing at a different theater than your favorite one. Do you still want to go?" Both theaters are two miles from your house.

Does the word *local* mean different things depending on where you live?

....

....

....

READ

Basic Local Community Needs

A person needs food, water, safety, and shelter. A community needs food, water, safety, and shelter too.

FOOD AND GOODS

The local economy needs ways for people to get food. That means there is a way to get food from the farms to stores where people can buy the food. The same is true for clothes, pencils, napkins, video games and any other products. Local economies have stores to sell products.

WATER AND SAFETY

The local economy needs ways for people to get water and power, and to be protected. Local governments provide **public utilities** (water, electrical, and/or gas systems) to all homes and businesses. Local governments also make sure **public safety** services such as police, fire, and emergency health care are available. Local economies provide public services.

SHELTER

Every community needs people who know how to build houses and buildings. The people who can build have special skills to provide services like carpentry, plumbing, and electrical work. A **skilled laborer** is anyone with special skills that are helpful to a community. Local economies have skilled labor.

PURPOSE

It is easy to understand the purpose of a community when we look at a small town. Some towns depend on the farms or ranches surrounding the town for food. Maybe a town's purpose comes from a mine, an oil field, or a factory. In larger communities, there are more choices in the kinds of jobs that produce goods and services. Local economies need a purpose.

The local economy benefits more when you buy locally made goods from local stores. The person who makes the good and the person who sells the good live in your community. Sometimes people make choices about what to buy just because it helps their neighbors in their community.

WRITE

What four things does a local economy need?

....

....

....

....

....

....

....

....

READ

Money

The **local economy** is the wealth and resources of a community. A healthy local economy provides ways to make money, use money, save money, and share money for important things.

Jobs are the way that people make money. Jobs produce things that people use (also called goods) or do things for people that are helpful (also called services).

People use money to buy the goods and services they need. When people spend money on goods and services, they are consumers.

A healthy economy saves money for the future. Banks allow people to keep their money in a safe place until they need it. In return for this service, people agree to let the bank use the saved money to lend to other people and businesses while they are not using it.

Did you ever wonder who pays the men and women who repair the streets? The local government pays them. Communities use taxes to do big and important things for the local economy. Taxes pay for police and fire departments, community health clinics, road construction and repair, and schools. That's just a few of the things taxes pay for.

WRITE

Where do people put money they want to save for later?

....

....

....

....

....

IN THE REAL WORLD

In the past, people had to go to the bank to get actual money to buy things or to save their money in an account. Today, many people prefer to do their banking by phone or computer and to use a card or phone for all their purchases.

PRACTICE

Use the word bank to identify the parts of a local economy.

Word Bank: bank   production job   public safety
                      public utility   skilled labor   store

1. ....

2. ....

3. ....

4. ....

5. ....

6. ....

REVIEW

In this lesson, you learned:

- An economy is the system in which money is earned and spent on goods and services.
- The amount of items that a store has to sell is its supply.
- If a lot of people want to buy an item all at once, this means the product is in demand.
- Buying locally is good for our local economy because the money stays in our community.

Think About It
How do the citizens contribute to the economy of a city or community?

Circle the correct answer.

1. A firefighter provides public _____.

   A. utility   **C.** access

   B. safety   **D.** parks

2. What is the system where people earn and spend money on goods and services called?

   A. economy   **C.** banking

   B. ecology   **D.** skilled labor

3. A local economy is the wealth and resources of _____.

   A. a nation   **C.** a community

   B. a country   **D.** an individual

4. People who train to do a special service like plumbing or carpentry are called _____.

   A. public servants   **C.** economists

   B. skilled labor   **D.** workmen

5. People use banks to _____ money.

   A. hide   **C.** spend

   B. print   **D.** save

ONLINE CONNECTION

With the help of your instructor, do an online search for hair salons within 25 miles of your location. How many salons are within five miles? How many salons are within 15 miles? How many are within 25 miles? Now repeat the exercise using the address of a family member who lives in a different environment. For example, if you live in a big city, choose a relative who lives in a small town. Compare your findings and discuss your discoveries with your instructor.

6. Local taxes pay for _____.

   A. police and fire protection   **C.** the Air Force

   B. national parks   **D.** helping other countries

7. Public utilities include _____.

   A. police stations

   B. fire stations

   C. water

Lesson 62

Economic Systems

By the end of this lesson, you will be able to:

- identify different organizations that are part of the economic systems (i.e., banks, small businesses, big corporations)

Academic Vocabulary

Read the following vocabulary words and definitions. Look through the lesson. Can you find each vocabulary word? Underline the vocabulary word in your lesson. Write the page number of where you found each word in the blanks.

- **bank:** a business where people deposit, withdraw, and borrow money (page ____)
- **bankers:** the people who run a bank (page ____)
- **corporation:** a legal entity that is separate from its owners (page ____)

TAKE A CLOSER LOOK

A currency is something exchangeable that makes the transfer of goods and services possible.

It is a form of money, and *money* is defined as a medium of exchange.

The smallest money ever used was called an *obol*. It was used in Greece and was smaller than an apple seed.

With the help of an adult, research how the people in Greece were able to use such a small item as currency.

Have you ever thought about how we get things? More often than not, we use money as a form of payment to get our basic needs or things that we want to use or have.

In the box below, draw a form of money that is used in your country.

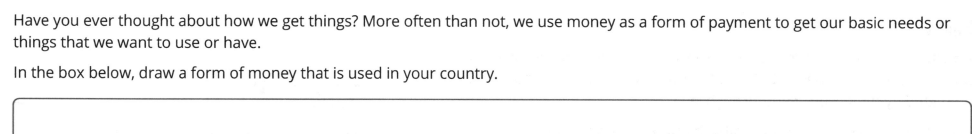

The United States has a market economy, which explains how the items that are produced, the things that are priced, and the things that are sold—as well as our investment in these things—are all based on supply and demand.

Supply refers to the quantity, or amount, of something that is available. *Demand* refers to what people want.

READ

Banks

A **bank** is a business where people deposit, withdraw, and borrow money. Banks also invest money to build up their reserve of money. What banks do is regulated by the government through laws.

The people who run a bank are called **bankers**. Certain banks deal directly with the public. Other banks only deal with investments and international currency trading.

A customer's money is placed in the bank for safety. Banks may give loans to customers for an agreement to pay the bank back at a later time. For example, people take out a mortgage loan from a bank to buy a home. Overtime, the people who took out the loan must pay back the bank in small payments until they have completely paid back everything they borrowed. However, there is usually an additional fee that is required as well—commonly referred to as an interest—that is added to the amount of money that the individual must pay back. This ensures that the bank receives the money they loaned back as well as makes it possible for the bank to continue giving loans to those who need it.

WRITE   What is the purpose of a bank?

....

....

....

....

....

READ

Corporations

A **corporation** is a legal entity that is separate from its owners. Corporations have most of the rights and responsibilities that individuals possess.

1. Corporations must enter contracts.
2. Corporations can loan and borrow money.
3. Corporations can sue and be sued.
4. Corporations can hire employees.
5. Corporations can own assets.
6. Corporations must pay taxes.

All kinds of businesses around the world use a corporate structure. Corporate shareholders may take part in the profits through dividends and stock appreciation, but they are not personally liable for the company's debts. Stock appreciation means the increase in the market value of stock.

Nearly all well-known businesses are corporations, including the Microsoft Corporation, the Apple Corporation, and the Coca-Cola Company.

WRITE

What is a corporation?

....

....

....

....

....

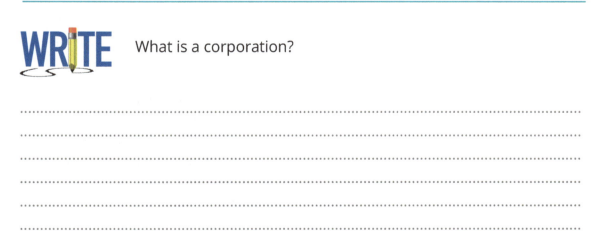

READ

Small Businesses

A small business is a privately owned company. It can be a corporation, partnership, or sole proprietorship. Small businesses have fewer employees and make less money compared to corporations.

Small businesses include service or retail operations such as convenience stores, small grocery stores, bakeries, salons, restaurants, small-scale manufacturing, and internet-related businesses like web design and computer programming. Other small-business examples include photographers, tradespeople (i.e., carpenters, electricians), lawyers, accountants, dentists, and medical doctors.

WRITE

Think about a small business in your neighborhood that you really like. What is the name of the small business, and why do you like it?

....
....
....
....

Compare and contrast a small business and a corporation.

....
....
....
....
....

REVIEW

In this lesson, you learned:

- A corporation is a legal entity that is separate from its owners.
- Most well-known businesses are corporations.
- A small business is a privately owned company that has fewer employees and makes less money than a corporation.
- A bank is a company where money can be saved or borrowed.

Think About It

What would happen if our economic system had no businesses? How would that impact you and your family? How would that impact our communities?

Circle the correct answer.

1. Choose the option that is part of our economic system but is not an organization.

A. banks

B. the free library book clubs

C. small businesses

D. big corporations

Use the words from the Word Bank to complete the sentences below.

Word Bank: corporation   small businesses   bank

2. A _____ is a legal entity that is separate from its owners.

3. _____ have fewer employees and make less money compared to corporations.

4. A _____ is a company where money can be saved or borrowed from.

Did you know that there are special bank accounts available for kids to open?

With the help of your instructor, research "bank accounts for kids" to learn about these accounts and how to get one. Discuss with your parents whether you should open your own bank account.

Lesson 63

Local Businesses

By the end of this lesson, you will be able to:

- identify three types of businesses
- describe how the local economy is effected by businesses opening and closing
- describe the benefits of local business ownership

Lesson Review

If you need to review how the economy works, please go to the lesson titled "Economic Systems."

Academic Vocabulary

Read the following vocabulary words and definitions. Look through the lesson. Can you find each vocabulary word? Underline the vocabulary word in your lesson. Write the page number of where you found each word in the blanks.

- **manufacturers:** businesses that make raw materials or finished products (page ____)
- **merchants:** someone who sells or trades goods to others (page ____)
- **recession:** a period when business slows down (page ____)

Essential Businesses

In March 2020, many people were getting sick from COVID-19. The government closed down places where people gathered and asked everyone to work from home if they could. However, some businesses could not close. Grocery stores, factories that made food, and farms had to stay open. Hospitals had to stay open. The police and fire departments were needed. The COVID-19 emergency made it clear that some businesses were absolutely necessary. Almost immediately, people started calling these businesses "essential businesses" and the people who worked at them "essential workers."

Almost every town and city has a chamber of commerce or something similar. A chamber of commerce is a local association that promotes and protects the interests of the local business community.

What can a chamber of commerce do? They might reach out to a company that builds truck stops and convince them to add a fueling station to one of their stops. The Chamber might help attract a car dealership, restaurant or factory, which would add more jobs to the community. They might convince the county to fund a community college that teaches necessary job skills. Everything a chamber of commerce does is meant to create more jobs in the local economy.

Why would a chamber of commerce invite people to shop in local stores? What does it mean to the owners of the stores? What does it mean for the workers in the stores?

....

....

....

....

....

....

....

....

Celebrating Essential Workers

In the early days of the COVID-19 crisis, the people of New York City found a way to say thank you to the essential workers. Each evening, at the same time, people would open their windows or go out on their fire escapes or balconies. They clapped, whistled, and cheered for all the workers risking their lives to keep the city open. Many other cities had similar celebrations across the world.

 **READ**

Types of Businesses

There are three types of businesses—manufacturing, merchandising, and service. **Manufacturers** are makers. They make raw materials or finished products. Miners, lumberjacks, farmers, and ranchers provide raw materials like coal, oil, metals, wood, food, fibers, and animals. Factories, mills, and processing plants turn the raw materials into goods for people to buy in stores.

Merchants are sellers. They sell raw materials and finished products. Some merchandisers buy raw materials like cotton and then resell these to manufacturers who make cloth or medical supplies. Wholesale merchandisers sell finished goods to other kinds of sellers. Retail merchandisers sell directly to the public.

Services are the third type of business. They fix items or do a task for people. Services can also create systems to support manufacturers and merchandisers. Health care workers are an excellent example. They diagnose health problems and help people heal. Computer technicians do the same thing for computers. Accountants create systems for keeping track of business expenses and profits.

Here are examples of each type of business.

Manufacturers	Merchants	Services
Agriculture	Real estate (sells land)	Finances (money)
Factories	Restaurants (sells to public)	Public safety
Mills	Retailers (sells to public)	Security (business safety)
Mining	Suppliers (sells to stores)	Transportation (ships, planes)
Processing plant	Wholesalers (sells to stores)	Utilities (power and water)

WRITE   What do merchants do?

....

....

....

....

READ

New and Old Businesses

Your local economy probably depends on a mix of local and national business. There may be a small factory in your town that makes circuit boards, which are shipped all over the world. Down the street, there might be a locally owned trucking company that transports the circuit boards across the country. In the next town, a car factory might be built, which requires many new workers. That might mean some of your neighbors may move there.

Competition for new businesses is fierce. When a new business opens, the community's economic health grows stronger, people in the community have more job opportunities, the business owner is invested in the community's overall success, and other related businesses might follow. However, when a business closes, workers may move to find new jobs, the community's pride and spirit suffer, and tax money moves to another community.

WRITE What would you do to support your community if you owned a local sporting goods store?

....
....
....
....
....
....
....
....

IN THE REAL WORLD

A recession is a period in which business slows. COVID-19 caused a worldwide recession. Many retail stores closed down for good. At the same time, internet stores did very well because people still needed to buy things. Shipping companies had to work hard to keep up. Eventually, though, many companies struggled to find the parts they needed to make new products. For example, one car needs between 24 and 36 microchips. New car production had to slow down because there were not enough microchips available. This made quality used cars more desirable, so the price of used cars went up. In a recession, it is normal for things to cost more because there are fewer things to buy and fewer people who can afford them.

Local Ownership

When a local person opens a business in their own town, several things happen. The new business:

- hires local people.
- pays local taxes.
- occupies an old, unused building or builds a new building.
- buys supplies locally.
- produces or sells local goods and services.
- donates to local causes (like sponsoring a youth soccer team).

 **WRITE**   List three good things about local businesses.

 **REVIEW**

In this lesson, you learned:

- There are three kinds of businesses: manufacturing, merchandise, and service.
- Opening a business is good for the local economy. Closing a business hurts the local economy.
- Locally owned businesses keep more money in the local economy.

Think About It

When the economy is not doing well, some goods like toys may be in short supply. If toys were in short supply, what could you do or play with instead that would not cost you any money?

SHOW WHAT YOU KNOW

Circle the correct answer.

1. Merchants _____ things.

   A. sell   **C.** recycle

   B. make   **D.** fix

2. Services _____ things.

   A. sell   **C.** recycle

   B. make   **D.** fix

3. Manufacturers _____ things.

   A. sell   **C.** recycle

   B. make   **D.** fix

4. Bread is a _____.

   A. raw material   **C.** recycled product

   B. finished product   **D.** service product

5. Accountants are _____.

   A. manufacturers   **C.** service providers

   B. merchants   **D.** apprentices

TAKE A CLOSER LOOK

Think about all of the ways you receive money, like gifts or maybe an allowance. What do you plan to spend your money on this week? Make a budget. The budget should include spending for goods and services, charitable donations, sales taxes, and saving.

Lesson 64

Chapter 12 Review

By the end of this lesson, you will:

- review the information from the lessons in Chapter 12, "Economic Systems."

Lesson Review

Throughout the chapter, we have learned the following big ideas:

- Producers make money selling goods and services to consumers. (Lesson 59)
- Banks lend money and protect money. (Lesson 60)
- A local economy is the wealth and resources of a community. (Lesson 61)
- Banks and businesses work together to form a local economy. (Lesson 62)
- Local businesses create local pride, local jobs, and local taxes. (Lesson 63)

Go back and review the lessons as needed while you complete the activities.

ONLINE CONNECTION

Different regions produce different things. What products are grown near you? Research online to find out about the different foods that are grown or raised in your area. Find out the following:

- the name of the crop or animal raised
- where the item is exported to
- popular dishes made with the crop or animal
- festivals celebrating the crop or animal (if there are any)

Share your research with your instructor.

REVIEW

Goods and Services

Goods are things. Goods are things you need or things you want. Goods are also called products.

Services satisfy a want or need. Services fix things or make them work well. Services do things you cannot do for yourself.

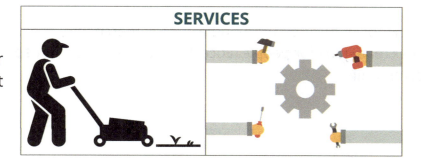

Consumers buy goods and services. Producers make goods and services. For example, a restaurant produces a meal. Consumers dine at the restaurant and eat the food. As a result, the employees get paid for the food and the restaurant owner pays the rent on the restaurant. This is how a business runs.

REVIEW

Local Economy

The local economy is the wealth and resources of a community. Communities are made of people working in businesses to create wealth and resources. The community uses tax dollars to ensure public safety, which provides the roads, water, and power necessary for people to live well and businesses to thrive.

Banks loan money to businesses so they can produce and to individuals so they can consume. Banks also provide services to help businesses and individuals to use money safely. Bank services include checking accounts, savings accounts, and investment accounts.

A local economy has three kinds of businesses: manufacturers, merchants, and services. These businesses create jobs for people. Local business ownership keeps the most money in the community.

WRITE

What kind of jobs are people proud of in your community?

....

....

....

....

....

PRACTICE

Vocabulary

Match each word in the Word Bank to each picture.

Word Bank: consumer   economy   manufacturer
                 service   public safety utility

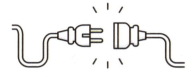

1. ....

2. ....

3. ....

4. ....

5. ....

6. ....

REVIEW

The word *economy* has two Greek root words. *Oikos* means "house." *Nemein* means "manage."

Oikos + Nemein = oikonomia

House + manage = manage the house

Maybe it is important to think of big ideas like the economy as being made up of smaller parts like managing our houses.

PRACTICE

Local vs. Nonlocal

LANA'S LOCAL MARKET		BUY BIG SUPERSTORE	
1 lb of locally grown organic carrots	$1.99	1 lb of carrots	$0.99
1 gallon of milk from local dairy	$4.49	1 gallon of milk	$2.49
1 loaf of fresh baked bread	$2.00	1 loaf of bread	$0.99
Total (with 5 percent tax)	$8.90	Total (with 5 percent tax)	$4.69

Lana's Local Market is owned by the Smith family. They live at the house on the corner of your street. Lana's husband, Mr. Smith, coaches The Blaze, a youth soccer team for third-grade girls and boys. Lana's Local Market pays for the team uniforms. The market also offers special prices on Saturdays on food that would otherwise go to waste.

Buy Big is a national chain of stores. Buy Big purchases the least expensive products they can find and passes the savings along to their customers. They also have frequent, unannounced sales to attract customers. Buy Big often advertises that they support various national charities.

 Which store will you pick and why? Discuss your answer with your instructor.

REVIEW

Sometimes businesses provide specialized services to generate income, which also helps them get repeat business.

For example, some fast food restaurants offer the service of providing birthday parties for children. This service includes Happy Meals, goodie bags for each child, invitations, placemats, party hats, birthday cake with candles, ice cream, and a special gift for the birthday child.

An employee sets up the party. This saves families a lot of time when planning a birthday party. This is one example of how companies provide valuable services to customers.

PRACTICE

Cause and Effect Relationships

Match the causes and effects in the chart below. There are exactly four causes and four effects.

- There is a truck driver shortage.
- People spend more time looking at online art exhibits.
- There are nine barbers in the community.
- Some stores run out of things to sell.
- Maria buys her own bicycle.
- The art museum closes temporarily.
- Some barbers lower their prices.
- Maria saves $5 a week.

CAUSE	EFFECT

Functions of Government and Economic Interdependence

Hi, there, my good friend!

I was at the United Nations with the U.S. president. For real!

Things were not going my way. I was trying to convince him to let us sell Mexican corn in the United States. He said farmers in the United States wanted to grow their corn.

I was not ready to give up.

I didn't know what to tell the president. Then, my cousin Juan came over with the Mexican president!

They were both so lovely to listen to two small grasshoppers. Juan said to both presidents, "We are better at growing corn in Mexico. It is a crop for warmer countries."

I nodded and said, "We are better at growing wheat in the United States. It is better for our colder weather."

Juan went on and said, "We need to grow what we are good at farming. That way, there will be better food." I added, "And it will cost less!"

The two presidents nodded. The Mexican president said, "You are right. In the end, everyone will be happier if we trade."

But the president of the United States was worried. "How do we convince corn farmers in Iowa that we should buy Mexican corn?"

We didn't know. But then my cousin Juan said, "I have an idea!" When I heard it, I knew it would work. Woohoo!

Do you want to hear what that idea is? Be ready, young grasshopper!

What Will I Learn?

This chapter examines how economies operate on the national level. It looks at how local economies and businesses fit into national economic systems of goods and services.

Lessons at a Glance

Lesson 65

Governments and Economies

By the end of this lesson, you will be able to:

- describe how government is important to the economic system
- identify examples of government involvement in local economic activities

Lesson Review

If you need to review the economy, please go to the lesson titled "Economic Systems."

Academic Vocabulary

Read the following vocabulary words and definitions. Look through the lesson. Can you find each vocabulary word? Underline the vocabulary word in your lesson. Write the page number of where you found each word in the blanks.

- **consumer:** people who buy goods or services (page ____)
- **economy:** the wealth and resources of a country or nation (page ____)
- **taxes:** money that people pay to the government to ensure the country can run properly (page ____)

Local Government

What is a local government? Local governments are the smallest form of government and manage cities or towns. They pass laws for their city, town, or county and provide services to people. These services include hospitals, police departments, and public works in charge of trash, sewer, road repair, and clean water. Mayors, city council members, and county commissioners, among other officials, help lead local governments. These are usually elected positions.

For a community to run, it needs people, laws, and an economy. Communities need people to be community helpers. Examples of community helpers are nurses, police officers, firefighters, waste management workers, and teachers. These community helpers are paid to help. The government funds many of these services. Citizens pay taxes to the local government to help pay for the services the community needs. Taxes help build the local economy. An **economy** is the wealth and resources of a country or nation.

Firefighters put out house fires, wildfires, and assist in medical emergencies.

Police officers enforce the laws of the government and respond to emergencies.

What are other community helpers in your town? What do they do? Does the local government fund them?

....
....
....
....
....

ONLINE CONNECTION

The government's economy assists many services, such as road building and emergency services. What is funded by the government differs from country to country. For example, not every country funds health care. In countries like the United States, people pay for their health insurance through their work or a private company. In Sweden, health care is primarily tax funded. Research what services your local government helps fund. Create a list of the services below.

....
....
....
....
....
....
....
....
....
....
....

READ

Why Is Government Important to the Economy?

Governments affect the economy in three ways: they offer goods and services, collect taxes, and manage economic activity.

Many governments offer services to their communities. The French government provides health care, education, and transportation. Their taxes fund these services. Also, these services create jobs for people. Other services governments provide are police departments, parks, and food assistance programs.

Money that people pay to the government is called **taxes**. These taxes are used to helpthe community by providing services. Taxes help pay for schools, roads, and libraries. The government decides how much a person will pay. They typically base it on how much money they make.

Construction workers laying a concrete road.

Governments oversee economic activities and put laws on those activities. These laws are to protect **consumers**, or those who buy goods and services, and the environment. One example of a law that protects consumers and the environment is a law that says companies are not allowed to dump garbage or waste into the ocean.

Where Does My Money Go?

In the United States, the government collects three types of taxes: sales tax, property tax, and income tax. Citizens pay income tax based on how much they earn. Property tax is based on the property they own (house, building, or land). Sales tax is based on goods or services citizens buy from a store or company. For example, a pair of pants may cost $10.00, but the final cost is $11.50. That little bit of extra money is the sales tax.

Pretend you bought a building for your new shop. You pay a percentage of its worth to the government. What type of tax is this?

WRITE

What are three ways the government affects the economy?

....
....
....
....
....

READ

Government and Local Economics

Governments use taxes to fund programs that affect local economies. For example, during the COVID-19 pandemic, many governments gave money to people and local economies. This extra money helped families purchase groceries and businesses stay open.

Another example is the government setting up assistance programs. In Mexico they have a social welfare program for low-income families. The program encourages families to send their children to school. The program's goal is to improve the poor's quality of life by providing nutrition, education, and health.

Merida town hall in Yucatan, Mexico

Many other countries have similar programs.

In Australia, people can apply for grants. These grants give people money for projects. Other countries do this as well. Donations from the government help small businesses and local improvements, such as new walking trails.

Sydney, Australia, town hall

Many countries' governments offer free public education. Free education creates jobs such as janitors, teachers, and office support. When a community has many jobs available, it helps grow the local economy.

CREATE

Draw your own pretend community. What would you call the community? What laws would you put in place? A community needs helpers, rules, and an economy. Include the following:

· your community name

· a detailed picture of the central area

· at least five laws

· at least three community helpers

· services the local government will offer

Also think about how the community will earn money. Will you tax the citizens? Will everyone be taxed the same, or will it be different depending on how much they make?

WRITE

Identify one way the government is involved in local economies.

....

....

....

....

....

PRACTICE

The government does get involved in local economic activities. This involvement helps raise the standard of living for the people in the community. In this lesson, you learned about the importance of government and the economy. You also learned about ways the government is involved in the local economy. Write three examples of how the government is involved in local economic activities. Fill out the graphic organizer below with your examples.

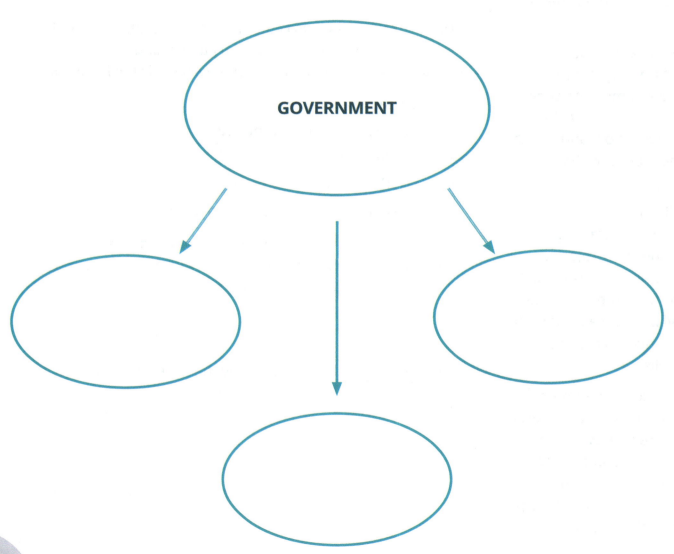

GOVERNMENT

Circle the correct answer.

1. Who are consumers?

   A. the economy

   B. people who buy goods or services

   C. people who create goods and services

   D. people who sell goods and services

2. What is an economy?

   A. the wealth and resources of a country or nation

   B. where money is created

   C. people who buy goods and services

   D. the money we give to the government

3. What are taxes?

   A. money that people pay to the government to ensure the country can run properly

   B. people who sell goods and services

   C. the wealth and resources of a country, town, or nation

   D. money people spend on what they need

4. Why is government involvement in local economies important? Circle all correct answers.

   A. they offer services

   B. they are not involved in any economies

   C. they collect taxes

   D. they manage economic activities

Germany's Government

Germany is one of Europe's most influential countries. Their government is a federal republic, meaning states have their own governments, yet they recognize the central government's rule. Germany has 16 states. They have limited government regulation, and their production of goods is based on supply and demand. The government does put limitations on production to protect its citizens and the environment. Germany's central government also provides health care and education for the states.

5. What are two examples of government involvement in local economic activities?

....

....

Lesson 66

Government Goods and Services

By the end of this lesson, you will be able to:

- identify goods and services provided by the government

Lesson Review

If you need to review governments and economies, please go to the lesson titled "Governments and Economies."

Academic Vocabulary

Read the following vocabulary words and definitions. Look through the lesson. Can you find each vocabulary word? Underline the vocabulary word in your lesson. Write the page number of where you found each word in the blanks.

- **goods:** items that people use or sell (page ____)
- **need:** something we must have to live (page ____)
- **services:** activities done to satisfy a want or need (page ____)
- **want:** something we would like to have but isn't necessary to live (page ____)

Needs and Wants

What is the difference between a need and a want? A *need* is something we have to have to stay alive. For example, we need water, shelter, and food to live. A *want* is something we would like to have but do not need to live. For example, toys, television, and decorations are all things we want. Do you think people should be given what they need? Whose job is it to provide those needs?

Dara and Henry created a lemonade stand. They are selling lemonade for 50¢ a cup. Their goal is to raise money to donate to their local animal shelter. Are Dara and Henry offering a service or a good? To answer, we need to know what those words mean. A **service** is an activity done to satisfy a want or need. As discussed previously, a **need** is something we have to have to stay alive while a **want** is something we would like to have but do not need to live. A **good** is an item that people use or sell because you want or need it. Dara and Henry offer a good to their customers because it is an item, not an action. People want lemonade, and they can purchase this good from the stand.

Now Dara and Henry are offering to mow lawns to raise money for the animal shelter. Think about it. Is cutting someone's lawn a service or good? It is a service because it is an action they are doing for someone else.

TAKE A CLOSER LOOK

A Service and a Good?

Can something be both a service and a good? Yes, things can be both. For example, a baker sells their baked items, which are goods, and they also bake items for you, which is a service. Another example is when a farmer grows and harvests food (which are services), then sells the food (or goods) to individuals and grocery stores.

READ

Goods and Services

Goods are something you buy or use. Food is a good because we use it. Crayons are goods because we use them. A service is an action a person does for someone else. Manicures, mechanic work, and childcare are all services.

Goods and services can be wants or needs. Purchasing a movie is a want and a good. Buying clothes is a need, and the clothes themselves are goods. Health care is a need and a service. Going to the hair salon is a want and a service.

Many governments assist people in meeting their needs. But if people want something, they must use their own money. The government provides some goods. Every country is different, so different goods are given to their citizens. Sometimes what the government offers a citizen depends on the person's income. Some governments provide services to the people living in their countries. Every country is different, so different services are offered to their citizens. Like goods, sometimes what the government offers depends on the person's income. Some services provided by the government are wants, but they raise the standard of living. For example, services like art classes or child activities help the entire community.

IN THE REAL WORLD

Many governments help people meet their basic living needs. As our world develops, new things are needed to be successful. Often students need the internet to be successful at school. Some local governments offer free internet to families in need so that students can do their schoolwork. The internet is needed so people can look for new jobs and learn new, necessary skills for the workforce too. Many governments also provide libraries, which offer computers and the internet for people to use. What do you think? Is the internet a need or a want? Talk to your instructor about your answer.

WRITE

What is a good or service your country offers to its citizens?

....

....

....

....

....

....

READ

Government Goods and Services Examples

Let us take a look at some examples around the globe.

The United States offers food stamps to people who have low income. Food stamps are given so that those people can purchase foods and basic needs. The United States also has a program called the Federal Housing Authority. This program provides both a service and a good. It aids Americans in becoming homeowners.

England provides low-income families with a food security program. This program allows people to be able to purchase foods and products that are essential needs. They also offer affordable housing to low-income individuals.

Japan offers its citizens public assistance programs to cover basic living expenses, housing costs, compulsory education and skill training costs, health insurance, and funerals. These programs offer goods and services provided by the Japanese government.

Tokyo, Japan

Sweden offers universal health care. This means that everyone has access to health care services like medical procedures and doctor visits. Sweden also provides social assistance for housing allowance, child allowance, and sickness coverage.

The Costa Rican government provides essential services to all its citizens. They provide safe drinking water, nutrition, and housing. They also offer all levels of health education for free to their people.

Russia offers social welfare. They provide unemployment, childcare, and healthcare assistance to those in need.

You may have noticed a similarity between all these countries. They offer help to meet the basic needs of the people living there. Most countries also offer public education, road maintenance, and emergency services like firefighters and police officers.

Stockholm, Sweden

PRACTICE

Label each thing as a service, good, or both on the first line. On the second line, write if it is a want or need.

Doll

....

....

Public Education

....

....

House

....

....

Swim Lessons

....

....

Coffee

....

....

Clothes

....

....

REVIEW

In this lesson, you learned:

- Goods are something you buy or use. Services are actions a person does for someone else.

- Goods and services can be needs or wants.

- Many governments assist people in meeting their needs.

Think About It

Do you think it is the government's role to provide its people with basic needs?

Circle the correct answer.

1. What is an example of a service?

  A. food   **C.** education

  B. water   **D.** clothes

2. What is an example of a good?

  A. car mechanic **C.** mail service

  B. sandwich   **D.** bus driver

3. What goods and services does Costa Rica's government provide? Select all that apply.

  A. drinking water **C.** nutrition

  B. cars   **D.** housing

4. What is an example of a need?

  A. toys   **C.** TV

  B. shelter   **D.** soccer ball

5. What is an example of a want?

  A. house cleaner **C.** clothing

  B. shelter   **D.** food

6. What is an example of both a service and a good?

  A. books   **C.** restaurant

  B. lemonade   **D.** car wash

Create an illustrated story about being stranded on an island. What items do you need? What services do you have to figure out? In your story, include five items you would need or want with you on this island. Be sure to indicate whether they are a need or a want. Also write about services you need. How will you take care of your health, and how will you stay warm and dry? Draw a picture to go along with your story.

Answer the following questions in complete sentences.

7. What goods and services does your country offer to people?

....

....

....

....

8. What is an example of a need that is a service?

....

....

....

....

Lesson 67

Taxation

By the end of this lesson, you will be able to:

- define the term *tax* and explain the relationship between taxation and government services

Lesson Review

If you need to review goods and services, please go to the lesson titled "Government Goods and Services."

Academic Vocabulary

Read the following vocabulary words and definitions. Look through the lesson. Can you find each vocabulary word? Underline the vocabulary word in your lesson. Write the page number of where you found each word in the blanks.

- **taxation:** when a government or authority places a tax on its citizens and businesses (page ____)
- **taxes:** money that people pay to the government to ensure the country can run properly (page ____)

IN THE REAL WORLD

How do the governments pay for the roads, education, and other services? The answer is taxes. Taxes are money that people pay to the government to ensure the country can run properly. Have you ever gone to the store to buy a shirt and the cost at checkout is more than the tagged price? This type of tax is sales tax. People pay the store the full amount, and the store passes the taxes on to the government. In Canada, there is a sales tax that is 5 percent of the purchase. England's sales tax is 20 percent of the purchase. In the Bahamas, they have no sales tax.

Communities need schools, roads, bridges, courthouses, and community helpers for it to run. To pay for those things, governments collect **taxes**. The three types of taxes are property, sales, and income. Not every place uses all these taxes. Even different regions of the same country may not use the same type of taxes. For example, there is no sales tax on purchases in the US state of Oregon, but there is in the state of Washington.

Sales tax is the additional money you pay when you purchase goods or services. Property tax is the money you pay to the government if you own land, property, or a building. Income tax is the money you pay the government based on the money you make.

When people do their property and income taxes, they fill out different forms. In the United States, these forms are due April 15th. In the United Kingdom, the tax forms are due January 31st. Here is a look at a US tax form.

Research your country. What are some things taxes pay for? For example, do they pay for schools, health care, and other social programs? Find three services or goods your nation provides and write them on the lines below.

1. ....

....

2. ....

....

3. ....

....

Image of 1040 Form from the U.S. Department of the Treasury is in the public domain.

What Is Taxation?

Taxation is when a government or authority places a tax on its citizens and businesses. Governments use the money they get from taxes to pay for things. For example, taxes pay government workers' salaries, such as the military and police force. Taxes also provide services such as education and health care and are used to build and repair roads, bridges, and sewers.

The three main types of taxes are sales, income, and property.

- Sales Tax: Sales tax is the additional money we pay to a store that is selling a good or service. For example, when people buy a car, a percentage of its worth is paid to the government.

- Property Tax: Property tax is the money we pay the government for any land or building we own. For example, if you won a piece of farmland, you would need to pay the government a percentage of its worth.

- Income Tax: Income tax is the money people pay to the government based on their earnings. The government decides the amount people pay. Jobs pay people who work for them. The money people make is then taxed based on a percentage of their total income. For example, the government may take 10 percent of a person's income.

Not every government uses all of these taxes. There may not be sales, property, or income taxes depending on where you live. For example, Fiji and Israel do not have property taxes but do have sales and income taxes.

 **REVIEW**

Governments use taxes to help improve and protect their nations. You have learned in previous lessons about the importance of government and the economy. You also learned about ways the government is involved in the local economy. The government manages economic activity, regulates companies, offers services and goods to people, and decides how much each person will pay in taxes.

WRITE What are the three types of taxes?

....

....

....

....

....

READ

Relationship Between Taxes and Government Services

To have economic growth, governments need a source of money for social programs and public investments. Programs providing health, education, and other services are important for a successful society. Taxes are what the government uses to pay for these services. All governments need income, which is why almost every nation has a tax system.

Governments should have a fair tax system. For instance, if governments use property tax to fund schools, different regions will receive different funding for education. People living in higher-property value areas will have more money for schools than those in low-property value areas. Governments need to make sure the money collected through taxes is equally distributed.

Taxes are a factor in what services are available to people. The higher the taxes, the more services the government can provide. The lower the taxes, the less the government can offer. There are pros and cons to both. Paying higher taxes means the individual has fewer choices on how they spend their money. Having higher taxes means more people have access to programs. In contrast, lower taxes give people less access to programs but more choice in spending their money.

IMPORTANCE OF TAXES

Taxes are needed to improve as a society. Taxes pay for other things like building and repairing roads, emergency services, and government buildings. Also, taxes pay for teachers, police officers, and firefighters.

WRITE

What is one benefit and one disadvantage of higher taxes?

....

....

....

....

....

....

....

....

....

PRACTICE

In the spaces provided, draw and write an example for each type of tax: sales, income, and property.

	SALES	INCOME	PROPERTY
Drawing			
Example			

REVIEW

In this lesson, you learned:

- The three types of taxes are property tax, income tax, and sales tax.
- Governments tax their citizens to pay for various government services, like the military, education, and health care.

Think About It

Do you think it is possible to have a balance between individual financial choice and government programs?

Choose the correct answer for each question.

1. What does the word *taxation* mean?

  A. money we donate to charities

  B. when a store asks for taxes from people

  C. when a government places a tax on its citizens and businesses

  D. when people do not pay their taxes

2. What do governments use taxes for? Circle all correct answers.

  A. education

  B. social programs

  C. amusement parks

  D. building and maintaining roads

3. What is one benefit of having lower taxes?

  A. more individual choice on how to spend money

  B. fewer social programs

  C. less access to programs

  D. more revenue for the government

4. What is one benefit of higher taxes?

  A. less individual choice on how to spend money

  B. more access to social programs

  C. more money for individuals

  D. more financial freedom for individuals

Research what type of taxes your country collects. What is the percentage of each tax? With the information collected, fill out the chart below.

Type of Tax	Does your country use it?	If yes, what percent?
sales		
property		
income		

Match each type of tax to its description.

5. _____ sales tax

6. _____ property tax

7. _____ income tax

A. the money we pay to the government based on our earnings

B. the money we pay to a store that is selling a good or service

C. the money we pay the government for any land or building we own

Lesson 68
Specialization

By the end of this lesson, you will be able to:

- identify local examples of specialization and division of labor

Lesson Review

If you need to review taxes, please go to the lesson titled "Taxation."

Academic Vocabulary

Read the following vocabulary words and definitions. Look through the lesson. Can you find each vocabulary word? Underline the vocabulary word in your lesson. Write the page number of where you found each word in the blanks.

- **civilization:** a group of people who live together with a government, similar culture, and a way of living (page ___)

- **division of labor:** when people share a workload by assigning tasks to each person (page ___)

- **game:** the common animals that are usually hunted in that area (page ___)

- **merchant:** someone who sells or trades goods to others (page ___)

- **migration:** the movement of people or animals, either for a short time or permanently, from one place to another (page ___)

- **scribe:** someone who writes or copies books (page ___)

- **specialization:** when a person concentrates on one job or task that can be done in the place where they live (page ___)

IN THE REAL WORLD

If you did not have any food in your house to eat, what would you do? Pretend that you must go out and find food. You can't steal food, but you also don't have any money. How would you find food to eat?

Discuss the following questions with your instructor:

1. Where would you go to get food?

2. Why is the food free?

3. Would you need to take anything with you to get the food?

4. How long could you eat food from this place before you had to travel somewhere else?

EXPLORE

Could you survive if you had to hunt and gather your own food? Let's find out!

1. You want to look for berries. Where would you look: in the middle of a forest, near a river, or in the plains?

   ....

   ....

   ....

2. You must make a spear to hunt for animals. How will you make your spear? What will you use to make it so that it will do its job well?

   ....

   ....

   ....

3. You are out walking around in the woods looking for food when you find mushrooms that look really yummy. The mushroom looks like the one in the picture. They have a red cap with white underneath the cap. You are very hungry. Would you eat this mushroom? Why or why not?

   ....

   ....

   ....

Look at the image of the animal below. Think about what parts of the animal hunters would use. They may be hunting the animals for more than just food. Why else would they be hunting? Are there any other animals they would also be hunting?

READ

History of Jobs

Many years ago, people did not have different jobs. Everyone moved around to different areas, always trying to find food. These people were called hunter-gatherers. Their days focused on finding enough food to survive. They hunted animals, picked berries, and gathered nuts they found on the ground. One group of people who did this were called the Paleo-Indians.

The Paleo-Indians used spears that they made from rocks to hunt for animals. They might hunt for bears, moose, or other game. The game is not playing cards or trying to win at an activity. Instead, **game** refers to the common animals that are usually hunted in that area.

It is believed that the Paleo-Indians migrated from Asia into Alaska approximately a few thousand years ago. **Migration** is the movement of people or animals, either for a short time or permanently, from one place to another. Because Alaska and Asia are so close, it is believed that they crossed between Russia and Alaska—known as the Bering Strait.

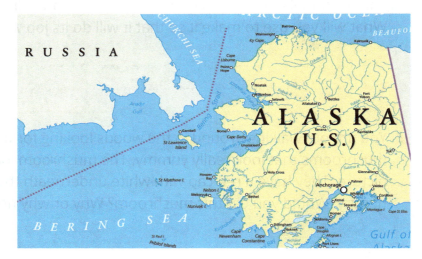

Paleo-Indians migrated in search of more food. They eventually traveled to Canada, the United States, Mexico, and South America. At first, these people continued to look for different animals to hunt and other food to eat. Then things began to change.

WRITE

Describe how the Paleo-Indians found food.

....

....

....

....

READ

Division of Labor

After the Paleo-Indians migrated to North and South America, many of them changed the way they lived. They stopped hunting and gathering for food, and some of them started farming the land. They settled and lived in one area, growing different types of crops. Some people might have hunted for animals, but then they might trade the meat for other things.

Since people were living in one place instead of moving around, they developed a civilization. A **civilization** is a group of people who live together with a government, similar culture, and way of living. In these civilizations, the people divided up the jobs that needed to be done. This became known as a division of labor. A **division of labor** is when people share a workload by assigning tasks to each person. These jobs could be farmers or hunters, but they could also be merchants, religious leaders, government leaders, soldiers, scribes, or teachers. A **merchant** is someone who sells or trades goods to others. A **scribe** is someone who writes or copies books. Since there were not any photocopiers around during this time, people had to write everything over again in order to make a copy.

Now people could focus on just one job. They would trade with their neighbors and other people in the city. For example, a farmer might grow corn or beans. He has plenty to feed himself and his family. However, he needs weapons to defend his land. He would trade his extra food to a merchant or soldier for a weapon.

CREATE

On a separate piece of paper, create a map showing what a civilization would look like. Include the division of labor by showing the different types of land on the map and the different jobs and buildings there.

You may want to include:

- farmland and farmers
- religious temples in the center of town
- buildings for scribes
- merchants in a marketplace

WRITE

How was living in a civilization easier than living as a hunter-gatherer?

....

....

....

....

Specialization

Even though people began to work only one job, they could not do whatever they wanted. It depended on where they lived. For instance, a farmer could not grow any kind of crop that they wanted. They could only grow what crops would thrive in that area's climate. This is because of specialization. **Specialization** means that a person concentrates on one job or task that can be done specifically in the place where they live.

Certain jobs are done today in specific areas of the world. With farming it is because certain climates and soil produce a specific type of crop. For example, the Midwest region in the middle of the United States grows a lot of wheat and other grains that are well-suited to the climate. China grows rice which needs a lot of water. In many areas of China, it rains a lot where the land is flat, so rice grows well there.

Besides farming, there are other types of jobs that are specialized in areas around the world. Silicon Valley in California is a good example. This is where people specialize in computers and technology. In Texas where they have found a lot of oil, many people have jobs mining for oil, rocks, and elements. Hawaii and Florida are two popular vacation destinations, so many people who live there work in hotels and restaurants.

The Midwest region of the United States is a great place to grow wheat.

China is a great place to grow rice.

Texas is a great place to drill for oil.

PRACTICE

Complete the graphic organizer about how the way people lived changed over time. Think about their movement, eating habits, and jobs.

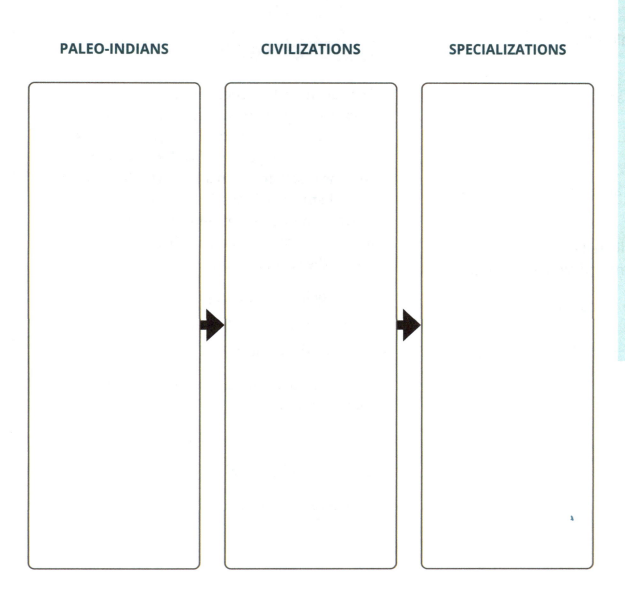

PALEO-INDIANS

CIVILIZATIONS

SPECIALIZATIONS

SHOW WHAT YOU KNOW

Use the words from the Word Bank to complete each sentence.

Word Bank: civilization   division of labor   game   rice   scribe
hunter-gatherers   migration   specialization

1. The Paleo-Indians are known as _____ because they hunted for animals and berries or nuts to eat.

2. The Paleo-Indians' _____ was a permanent movement from Asia to Alaska.

3. _____ are the common animals that are usually hunted in that area.

4. The Paleo-Indians stayed in one place and established a _____ with a government and similar culture.

5. A _____ is when people focus on one type of job.

6. One type of job was a _____, who wrote or copied books.

7. _____ means that a person concentrates on one job or task that can be done in the place they live.

8. China specializes in growing _____ in flat and wet land.

ONLINE CONNECTION

Did you know that there are groups of people who still migrate to different areas to live? They are called nomads. Today, some tribes move around to get food just like the Paleo-Indians did. Some nomads herd their animals with them to their destinations while others move in more modern vehicles. To learn more about nomads today, research and learn about one of the groups below:

- the Kochi people in Afghanistan
- the Sami people in Russia
- the Gaddi people in India

As you research these nomads, think about these questions:

1. How do they get their food?

2. Why do they move?

3. Where do they go?

Lesson 69

Trade

By the end of this lesson, you will be able to:

- identify examples of trade, imports, and exports in a community

Lesson Review

If you need to review specialized jobs, please go to the lesson titled "Specialization."

Academic Vocabulary

Read the following vocabulary words and definitions. Look through the lesson. Can you find each vocabulary word? Underline the vocabulary word in your lesson. Write the page number of where you found each word in the blanks.

- **barter:** to trade (page ____)
- **export:** to take items or goods to another country or place to trade or sell (page ____)
- **import:** to bring items or goods into a country or place from outside of the country of place (page ____)

IN THE REAL WORLD

Can you think of a time when you traded something you had with a friend? Describe what you got. Describe what you gave to your friend. Do you think it was an even trade? This means that both objects that were traded were of the same value. Sometimes trading is not an even trade. One side might get more than the other side. Why would someone trade for something less valuable than what they are providing to the other person?

EXPLORE

Dig through your toys. Find one that you don't want to play with anymore. Think about what you would trade it for. Then look at the picture. There are many toys and interesting things in the picture. Choose one toy or item in the picture that you would trade for your toy. Do you think it is a fair trade? This means that both items are worth about the same amount. Is the item you will get worth more money or is the item you are giving away worth more money?

....

....

....

....

....

....

Shipping Goods

In this picture, there are many big boxes on this ship. Each box is the same size. What do you think is in the boxes? There are probably goods and products in these boxes. Why do you think a ship like this would be carrying these large shipping boxes? Why isn't an airplane flying a few of these boxes at a time? If these boxes are coming into a country, where do you think they came from? Discuss your ideas with your instructor.

READ

Trade in a Community

Historically, people had to trade for things that they needed. They did not have money. The people in a community would barter mostly with the other people within the community. **Barter** means to trade. Due to the division of labor, different people did different jobs. Each person could make a good or perform a service and then trade with other members of their community for things they needed.

For example, farmers who grew corn in their communities grew enough food for themselves and their families. However, they most likely grew extra corn. They would take this corn to the market in the center of town to trade with other families. Another family might have needed corn but grew beans. The families who grew corn would trade with the family who grew beans. Families traded other things that were not food. These things included clothing, fur, weapons, and books.

Usually, towns had a place where many people came together. This place was the town center. The town center hosted many community events including trading. Today, we use money to buy things and don't trade necessities. Even though we have money, people still sometimes trade in the United States. Children often trade toys or baseball cards.

Trades should be fair.

IN THE REAL WORLD

People do not have to trade if they don't want to. In some cases, the two items that are being traded are not worth the same amount of money. In this situation, someone would get a good deal and someone would get a bad deal. For example, a child could trade a baseball card worth $1 for a baseball bat worth $25. One person would get something worth a lot more than what they are giving up. Sometimes people will trade something worth a lot more because they need the other item, in which case they would not consider it a bad deal.

WRITE

How would people trade with each other in a community?

....

....

....

....

READ

Imports in a Community

Sometimes in a community, some items are not available. It could be that certain crops don't grow in that area. The climate or soil may not support growing that type of crop. Certain minerals only exist in certain places. Therefore the citizens in other regions would be without those things. They can't trade for those items in the community because nobody makes or grows them.

The people must then import the items that they need. **Import** means to bring items or goods into a country or place from outside of the country or place. When these items are imported, they usually cost more money. They must be shipped or brought by merchants to the community.

We see this today. In your community, people import goods. These goods cost more money. They could be cars, food, or electronics. Today, it doesn't take as long to get these imported goods to our communities as it did many years ago. The United States imports certain things that are not produced domestically. Oil, spacecraft, and helicopters are some examples of products that the United States imports.

WRITE

How would you know if a toy you bought was imported?

....

....

....

....

....

....

Importing Goods

Many items are imported into a country. This means that these goods or products are not made within that country. It could be because people don't know how to make these products or they can't make them with the tools or supplies that they have. Look at the picture. These boxes are being imported into the United States.

How do you know that the goods or products were not made in a community in the United States but instead are being imported?

READ

Exports in a Community

Just like people need things that they don't have, they often also have extra of what they do create. They don't want to throw away the goods, so they export them. **Export** means to take items or goods to another country or place to trade or sell.

Throughout history, people built roads for trading. They would even sell or trade their extra goods along the side of the road as they traveled. However it was still difficult and dangerous to travel long distances to export their goods.

Today, individuals do not export the extra goods they produce. This is because they usually work for companies. The companies export the goods to other countries or communities. Some examples of goods exported from the United States are airplanes, cars, car parts, machines, and equipment.

PRACTICE

Read each situation. Then write the word that describes that situation (trade, import, or export).

SITUATION	WORD
A company in another country sells electronics to a company in your community.	
A boy gives his friend his bike, and his friend gives him a beanbag chair.	
A factory makes cars and sells the rest to a company in another country.	

REVIEW

In this lesson, you learned:

· People trade goods and products within a community. People trade with each other because people can give up something and need something in return.

· If a company or community imports goods, it means the people in the community need those items and the community can't provide them.

· If a company or community exports goods, it is because the company makes too many goods to sell only within their community or country. They sell the extra goods to companies or communities in another country.

Think About It
How is trading within a community better than trading outside of a community?

Circle True or False.

1. True or False   Barter is another word for trade.

2. True or False   Often in the United States people trade baseball cards for other sports items.

3. True or False   One main export of the United States is oil.

4. True or False   The United States often exports cars to other countries.

5. True or False   Export means to sell products to only people in your own community.

6. True or False   The United States exports airplanes to other countries.

7. True or False   The United States makes a lot of spacecrafts to sell to other countries.

8. True or False   Import means to buy products from other communities or countries.

ONLINE CONNECTION

Research the most famous trading area in history. Look for a map of the Silk Road. Merchants traveled the Silk Road for hundreds of years. They would sell their products all along the 4,000 mile (6,437.4 kilometer) route. Most of the merchants wanted to get to China to trade their goods for silk. That is where the name "Silk Road" originated. Research more about where the merchants came from and what they most likely traded.

Lesson 70

Chapter 13 Review

In this lesson, you will:

- review the information from the lessons in Chapter 13, "Functions of Government and Economic Interdependence."

Lesson Review

Throughout the chapter, we have learned the following big ideas:

- Trading and bartering occurred among the people within a civilization. (Lesson 66)
- Government and economics go together. (Lesson 67)
- Government raises funds through taxation. (Lesson 67)
- Civilizations were established by hunter-gatherers settling down. (Lesson 68)
- Importing and exporting are important in communities.(Lesson 69)

Go back and review the lessons as needed while you complete the activities.

PLAY.

Pretend to trade something like a toy or food. Think of what people hundreds of years ago would trade. How do you think people from hundreds of years ago would negotiate a trade? What do you think they would need to trade? Finally act out the trade.

Discuss your ideas with your instructor.

REVIEW

Government and Economics

The economy is the wealth and resources of a country, town, or nation. The government assists people who can't get a job or provide food for their families. There are programs offered by the government to help families if they apply. Some of these programs include providing extra money or resources to families. Often programs provide money for food to feed the families. Other assistance programs help the adults in a family get a job.

These programs cost money so the government must collect money through taxes. Taxes are the money that people pay to the government to ensure the country can run properly. A small amount of the taxes collected goes toward these assistance programs. Some taxes fund agencies that supervise companies to make sure they are following the laws. Taxes also pay for public services like police and fire departments.

Consumers are people who buy goods or services. A good is something you purchase or use, whereas a service is an action someone else does for you. A good can be held but a service cannot. Some goods could be toys, televisions, and books. Services could be medical procedures, childcare, and education. Some goods and services are needs like food, water, and shelter. Some goods and services are wants, things people would like to have but they do not need them to live. An example of wants could be toys.

A public assistance program like food assistance requires a lengthy application process. To qualify, an adult in the family must fill out an application. The application asks for information about all the money the family receives each month. The family applying may also need to list their bills and expenses. Finally, the application will ask for the number of children in the home. After the family submits the application, an employee working for the program will review the application and ensure everything is correct. The program determines if the person qualifies or not. If the person qualifies, the program determines how much money or goods the family will receive each month based on the family's needs.

Describe a time when you went to a store and bought a good or service. What was the cost of the good or service? Include how much you paid, including taxes.

REVIEW

Taxation and Migration

Taxation is when a government or authority places a tax on its citizens and businesses. The taxes are used to pay for public services and provide money for public assistance programs. The taxes received by the government is the money that people pay to the government to ensure the country can run properly. They may pay for the military, schools, and healthcare.

There are three types of taxes. These are property tax, sales tax, and income tax. Property tax is the money people pay the government for any land or building that the person owns. Sales tax is the money people pay to a store that is selling a good or service. Income tax is the money people pay to the government based on their earnings.

Hundreds of thousands of years ago, people called the Paleo-Indians had to hunt and gather for food. The Paleo-Indians lived in Asia and migrated to America. They established civilizations when they settled their new land. Once the Paleo-Indians started living together in one location, they created their own government, culture, and way of living. They divided jobs among themselves based on each person's talent. Therefore, some people were farmers and grew the food for the rest of the people in the civilization. Meanwhile, other people made other useful products for the community. When a person concentrates on one job or task that can best be done in the place where they live, that is called specialization. When people focus on one type of job, that is called a division of labor.

WRITE Why do you think civilizations were created?

....

....

....

If a consumer who likes to spend money buys more of their wants than needs, they may run out of money by the end of the month. Many people budget their money. A budget includes a list of things that should be paid first each month. The leftover money can be spent on the wants. If they do not pay for their needs like water or electricity, the electricity or water company will shut off the service. The consumer must pay to have it turned back on. In addition to the inconvenience of being without water or power, the person may have to pay extra to turn it back on, so it is good to have a budget.

PRACTICE

Category Words

Look at the Word Bank below. Split the words into three groups that each have something in common. Label each group based on what those words have in common.

Word Bank: books   shelter   food assistance
                 toy   electricity   televisions
                 water   parks   police department

1. _____

   A. _____

   B. _____

   C. _____

2. _____

   A. _____

   B. _____

   C. _____

3. _____

   A. _____

   B. _____

   C. _____

REVIEW

When an employee first begins a job, they fill out some forms. This allows different amounts of taxes to be withdrawn from each employee's paycheck. This form also shows how much money the employee makes as well as how many children the employee supports. The information on the forms lets the company know how much tax to take out of the paycheck and send to the government.

PRACTICE

Types of Taxes

Of the three kinds of taxes, explain which type of tax you and other children pay most. Why would you pay more of that type of tax than the others? In a paragraph, explain why children pay that tax more than other types of taxes.

....

....

....

....

....

....

....

....

....

....

....

....

....

....

....

REVIEW

When civilizations were first established, they needed scribes to copy information for many people to access. Some civilizations, like the Aztecs, had a very big population, so it wasn't easy to get information to so many people. Therefore scribes needed to write and rewrite the information. Once enough copies were made, the information was distributed around the civilization. Do you think you would enjoy a job like this?

PRACTICE

Cause and Effect

Read the sentences below. Then write the cause or effect of each situation.

CAUSE	EFFECT
Paleo-Indians were hungry.	
	A soldier traded his sword for enough corn to feed his family.
A company sold their goods to the community, but they have many goods left over.	

WRITE Think about your learning. What stands out to you in the lessons? What questions do you have? What do you wonder about? You can use this page to take notes, write out your responses, and then discuss them with your instructor.

Chapter 14
Income, Profit, and Wealth

Hi! It is Julia, the grasshopper here!

My cousin Juan and I went to the United Nations. We wanted to convince the leaders of the world to trade. We wanted to be allowed to trade American wheat for Mexican corn.

We must have done a good job. We convinced the presidents of both the United States and Mexico! They were both worried. The farmers growing corn in the United States might not like it if we trade for corn with Mexico. The U.S. farmers might be out of a job.

Juan had an idea. Be ready, young grasshopper!

The two presidents listened to Juan's idea. They invited corn farmers in the United States to talk to them. We were invited too!

The farmer's leader is named Doug. He said he had to feed his family, and it would cost a lot of money to plant wheat instead of corn.

The U.S. president said, "We have an offer for you, Doug. We will give you the money you need to remove the corn and plant wheat instead. Mexico and other countries will buy it from you. As a result, you will have more customers than before."

Doug was happy and said, "That sounds fair." So now food is cheaper and better for everyone.

Fun fact: When everyone works hard and cooperates, everyone wins. Woohoo! Another fun fact: Even small grasshoppers can change the world and make it better. And if we can, so can you! Woohoo!

What Will I Learn?

This chapter looks at the private sector of the economy. It examines the motivations of employees, entrepreneurs, and individuals who save money.

Lessons at a Glance

Lesson 71

Why People Work

By the end of this lesson, you will be able to:

- explain why people work
- describe the differences in earnings by those in different jobs

Lesson Review

If you need to review the importance of money in everyday life, please go to the lesson titled "Money and Banks."

Academic Vocabulary

Read the following vocabulary words and definitions. Look through the lesson. Can you find each vocabulary word? Underline the vocabulary word in your lesson. Write the page number of where you found each word in the blanks.

- **currency:** money used in a certain area (page ___)
- **economy:** the wealth and resources of a country or nation (page ___)
- **goods:** items that people use or sell (page ___)
- **interdependence:** two or more people or things that rely on each other (page ___)
- **labor:** work exchanged for money (page ___)
- **need:** something we must have to live (page ___)
- **occupations:** jobs (page ___)
- **services:** activities done to satisfy a want or need (page ___)
- **trade:** the transfer or exchange of goods and services (page ___)
- **want:** something we would like to have, but isn't necessary to live (page ___)

Imagine someone told you to pretend to be at work. What would you do? Why do people go to work, and what do they do there? Have you ever seen someone at work?

EXPLORE

Brainstorm a list of the different jobs and businesses in your community. Think about the number of working people you run into in a typical week and who they are. What jobs do they do?

JOB TITLE	WHAT THEY DO

TAKE A CLOSER LOOK

Types of Jobs

What jobs do people do in your neighborhood? Have you seen people delivering packages, painting fences, or selling goods? What other jobs would you add to the list?

READ

Why People Need Money

As kids grow up, they may start paying for some things. Eventually, they become adults and pay for all their own food, clothes, cars, and vacations. As people grow older, they start to need and want more, and they start to work to earn money.

Trading and bartering may have worked long ago, but today, we need money. Imagine trying to trade a toy car for a bag of carrots at a store! We use money for everything. We use money to buy the goods and services we want and need. **Services** are activities done to satisfy a want or need, such as the doctor treating people who do not feel well. **Goods** are items that people use or sell.

Everyone has basic **needs**, or things we must have to live. We need food, water, and shelter. If we break a leg, we go to a doctor because we also need to be healthy. A **want** is something we would like to have, but is not necessary to live. We want toys and games. We trade our skills to get money for the things we want and need.

Money is also called currency. **Currency** is the money in a certain area. For example, the paper bills and coins you use to buy things are currency. People have **occupations**, or jobs, where they are paid to work. **Labor** is work exchanged for money. Workers use the money to buy the things they need and want. If we do not have enough money, we cannot buy that item.

What If Money Did Not Exist?

Money did not always exist. People used to trade for things they needed. Could we go back to living that way? If money did not exist, we would probably only trade or barter for what we needed to live. We need food, clothing, and shelter. How could we get these essentials?

What do you think would happen if money did not exist? Talk to your instructor about your answer.

READ

Communities Need Workers

Members of a community exchange goods and services to make sure everybody has what they need. An **economy** is the wealth and resources of a country or nation, and it requires many people for the system to be successful.

People work to make money. Then they can buy groceries and other necessary supplies. The store owners use the money they make from selling to buy more products to restock the shelves. Farmers and ranchers produce food and mills make items for stores to sell. All of these actions are related and dependent on each other. If something happens to one of these parts, everyone is affected. All community members rely on each other to have a successful economic system. This buying, selling, and working is known as **trade**, and it's a big part of our economy.

We need people to make clothes, harvest fruit and vegetables, and care for sick people. Someone has to run the gas stations, post offices, stores, and banks. Society depends on us all working together. This is called **interdependence**. In an economy, all parts depend on each other doing their role.

People earn different amounts of money to do their jobs. Some people earn millions of dollars. Others earn thousands, even though they work the same number of hours day by day. Many times, several people who do the same job earn different amounts of money. How much a person earns depends on where they live, how hard the job is, what training they have, and how long they have been doing the work.

ONLINE CONNECTION

Some jobs have huge wage differences. An MLB athlete makes a lot more than a player in the minor leagues. A performer on a world tour earns a lot more than a person playing a guitar in a cafe. When you choose a career, check out the top, average, and bottom earners for a better idea of the range. With your instructor's help, go online and look up the average salaries of your top three dream jobs. How different are they? Is there a range of salaries within that career?

PRACTICE

1. What is one reason people need money?

....

....

2. What is one reason people work?

   A. to buy services   **C.** to pay employees

   B. to pay banks   **D.** to buy money

3. How do people get money?

   A. They buy it from a store.   **C.** They earn it from a job.

   B. They print it at home.   **D.** They buy it from a bank.

4. What has no effect on how much someone is paid?

   A. the business's location   **C.** the worker's clothing

   B. how long they've done the job   **D.** how well they do the job

5. What does the word *labor* mean?

....

....

6. Write about a job you could do now at your age and how much you might earn.

....

....

....

....

In this lesson, you learned:

- People need money to pay for their wants and needs.
- People use money to buy goods and services.
- People do work or labor to earn money.
- If money didn't exist, it would be more difficult to get what we want.
- Everyone in a community relies on each other to work.
- Many factors affect how much people earn at their jobs.

Think About It

Can you make a list of everything in your home that costs money? What are some things you should consider when choosing a career?

Show WHAT YOU KNOW

Circle the correct answer.

1. Which of the following is a job a third-grader could do for money?

   A. taxi driver

   B. bank teller

   C. sailor in the navy

   D. small dog walker

2. What is an occupation with a big difference in the wages of the people who do it?

   A. trash collector

   B. limo driver

   C. math teacher

   D. sports player

3. Which of the following is most likely the highest earner?

   A. a stay-at-home parent

   B. an owner of a busy restaurant

   C. a third-grader at their first job

   D. a server in a slow restaurant

4. Which is an example of interdependence?

   A. a parent who relies on a neighbor to watch her son so she can work

   B. a child who plays in a backyard, so he doesn't have to go to school

   C. a worker who takes a break because the workday is long and tiring

   D. a teenager who wants a job but isn't yet old enough to do any jobs

TAKE A CLOSER LOOK

Kids Can Have Jobs Too!

Do you have chores at home? Do you get an allowance? What can you do for money? Do you live in a busy neighborhood? Kids have been making money with lemonade stands for many years. Other options are shoveling snow, raking leaves, and cutting grass. Think about things you can do to make money. You could walk small dogs, wash cars, or weed someone's garden. Maybe you could make a deal with the grownups in your house to do chores for some spending cash. Some parents pay their kids a weekly allowance for keeping up with their household chores.

Match the term to the example of it.

5. _____ good   A. game creator

6. _____ service   B. video games

7. _____ needs   C. walking a dog for $10

8. _____ wants   D. food and shelter

9. _____ occupation   E. dollars and cents

10. _____ currency   F. a book for school

11. _____ labor   G. house cleaning

How Businesses Meet Needs and Wants

By the end of this lesson, you will be able to:

- describe how different businesses meet the needs and wants of families

Lesson Review

If you need to review the importance of working, please go to the lesson titled "Why People Work."

Academic Vocabulary

Read the following vocabulary words and definitions. Look through the lesson. Can you find each vocabulary word? Underline the vocabulary word in your lesson. Write the page number of where you found each word in the blanks.

- **advertising:** materials made to convince people to buy a product or service (page ____)
- **capitalize:** to take a chance at making money (page ____)
- **consumers:** people who buy goods or services (page ____)
- **desirable:** something that is wanted by many people (page ____)
- **interdependence:** two or more people or things that rely on each other (page ____)
- **producers:** people who make goods or offer services (page ____)
- **specialization:** focusing on one thing (page ____)
- **trade:** the transfer or exchange of goods and services (page ____)

CREATE

Close your eyes and think about your neighborhood. What are some of the most important businesses in your neighborhood? Where do your parents go often? Where do you go? Draw a small map of your town, noting all of the businesses. Draw an icon that helps you know what each business is (like a tooth for the dentist's office).

Almost every family spends time at the grocery store every week because all human beings need food. People rely on their neighborhood stores to have everything a family might need. We can all live pretty peacefully, knowing that if we ever need anything, we can drive a few miles and grab it. But what if you entered the grocery store and the shelves were empty? How would your family make dinner that night? You could go to a restaurant, but what if that were closed too?

You rely on the stores and businesses in your neighborhood to be open and stocked. You rely on the electric company to pump electricity into your house so you can have lights.

But did you know that those stores and businesses rely on you too?

In a neighborhood, businesses and people need each other. When did a local business or store really help you?

....

....

....

....

....

....

Why do you think your neighborhood businesses need you?

....

....

....

....

Why Families Need Business

Families want to feel safe and happy. Businesses sell goods and services to help families feel that way. Great businesses sell the exact goods and services that many different people want to buy. When that happens, businesses earn money, and people buy what they want and need.

Producers are the people who make goods or offer services. **Consumers** are the people who buy goods or services. Producers want to earn money from the things they make. Producers spend a lot of time figuring out what consumers want to buy. Producers and consumers are important to each other. Producers need to make and sell things that the consumer wants.

Producers develop goods for different reasons. Some producers love making something so much that they decide to sell it. Other producers focus on gaps in the market. They see a problem, and they think of ways to fix the problem. They solve consumers' problems with their goods and services. Other producers look at what is selling and make something similar. They might do it cheaper or in a different way. They look for ways to **capitalize**, or take a chance at making money, by selling items that are already popular. Some things are more **desirable** (this means many people want them), so they cost a lot of money. All these approaches are important because they give consumers more choices.

TAKE A CLOSER LOOK

A fad is something that many people love and admire but only for a short time. A common saying is, "That's just a fad!" Fads are popular, so they are often expensive and difficult to find in stores. However, people grow tired of fads pretty quickly. Once a fad loses popularity, the items usually end up on sale for a low price. Sometimes people think something is a fad, but it ends up staying popular for a long time.

READ

Trade and Specialization

The transfer or exchange of goods and services is called **trade**. When you buy a new pair of jeans at a store, you affect a lot of people. You get the new jeans you want and the shop earns money. They pay the producer to make the jeans and pay an employee to sell the jeans. Shipping companies make money moving the jeans around the country. Trade creates a lot of jobs!

Trade leads to **specialization**, or focusing on one thing. Trade allows us to focus on doing the things we do well and using money to trade for the rest of what we need. Specialization allows producers to improve, which leads to better products for everyone. This system connects people in a community through **interdependence**. The entire world is connected by labor, resources, and finished products.

Trade is a system that has many connected parts. An example of trade is making jeans. A factory needs a variety of resources. A farmer specializes in growing cotton, harvesting it, and selling it. Another company turns the cotton into cloth and dyes it. The jeans company moves the fabric to a factory where people and machines cut and sew the fabric. Other people focus on **advertising**, or convincing the public to buy a product. Some businesses display the jeans and help customers find a pair that fits. It takes a lot of different people and resources to get just one pair of jeans to the person who needs them.

ONLINE CONNECTION

Go online and search for a product to buy. Look at the competing products. How does each one distinguish itself from the other? How does each producer try to get your attention? How different are the products from each other? Do we need that many choices for a single type of product? Talk to your instructor about your findings.

PRACTICE

On the line under the image, explain how the business is meeting the wants and needs of families.

1. ....
....
....

2. ....
....
....

3. ....
....
....

4. ....
....
....

Discover! SOCIAL STUDIES • GRADE 3 • LESSON 72

Circle the correct answer.

1. What is a way that producers come up with goods and services? Circle all correct answers.

A. They buy an idea from the internet.

B. They love doing something so much they want to make it their job.

C. They solve a problem for the consumer.

D. They give consumers money for their product ideas.

E. They make something similar to what's already selling well.

F. They create a problem for the consumer.

2. Which of the following is a producer?

A. a bank

B. a school

C. a bakery

D. a hospital

3. Which of the following is a consumer?

A. someone who builds

B. someone who writes a mystery novel

C. someone who buys food

D. someone who makes ice cream

4. Which of the following is not something everyone needs?

A. clean water

B. clean air

C. healthy food

D. eyeglasses

IN THE REAL WORLD

What business does your family use most? What kind of business is it? What does your family buy there? Go visit the business and let the employees know they are doing a good job. If you can't visit, send them a letter or online message. Tell them you are learning about businesses and you think they do a good job serving your family.

Use the Word Bank below to fill in the blanks.

Word Bank: desirable   capitalize   advertising

5. Producers let consumers know about their product through _____.

6. The more _____ an item is, the more money can be charged for it.

7. Entrepreneurs sometimes _____ on an already popular item.

8. What is interdependence? How is your family interdependent on each other?

....

....

....

....

....

....

....

....

....

Entrepreneurship

By the end of this lesson, you will be able to:

- define the word *entrepreneurship*
- list examples of entrepreneurs in the local community

Lesson Review

If you need to review how businesses help meet the needs and wants of their customers, please go to the lesson titled "How Businesses Meet Needs and Wants."

Academic Vocabulary

Read the following vocabulary words and definitions. Look through the lesson. Can you find each vocabulary word? Underline the vocabulary word in your lesson. Write the page number of where you found each word in the blanks.

- **capital resources:** tools, items, buildings, or goods required to provide goods and services (page ____)
- **employee:** someone who works at a business (page ____)
- **entrepreneur:** a person who uses resources to become a producer (page ____)
- **entrepreneurship:** the act of using productive resources to produce a good or service to make a profit (page ____)
- **human resources:** people who work to provide a good or a service (page ____)
- **productive resources:** things a person needs to become an entrepreneur, such as resources, human resources, capital resources, and entrepreneurship (page ____)
- **profit:** the money left over after an entrepreneur pays for all of the resources it takes to produce a good or service (page ____)
- **resource:** something used for a purpose (page ____)

ONLINE CONNECTION

What is a product that you love? It can be something you own or something you wish you owned. Do some research online. Who created the product? What is the cost of the product? Are there any similar products being sold? What makes the one you want special?

EXPLORE

Have you ever thought about running your own business? Here are some facts about owning a business:

- Only about 10 percent of Americans own their own businesses. Most people earn money by working for someone else's company.
- A business does not have to be big. You can run a one-person business that does not have employees.
- Many businesses are owned and run by families. These businesses are often passed down to the children of the family.
- Small businesses make up a huge part of our economy and provide jobs to many people.

Imagine you were the big boss, the head honcho, the main person in charge with all eyes looking at you for leadership. What would be great about being your own boss? What would not be fun about being your own boss? Why do you think so few people want to be their own boss?

....
....
....
....
....
....
....
....

IN THE REAL WORLD

Imagine there were no more jobs available and you had to start your own business. What kind of business would you open? Remember that the number one reason that businesses fail is that customers don't want or need what they're selling. How would your business overcome that obstacle?

What Is Entrepreneurship?

Did you know a worker can become a business owner? Many businesses start small. Eventually, they can hire employees if the business grows. A person who uses resources to become a producer is called an **entrepreneur**.

Productive resources are the things a person needs to become an entrepreneur. They don't need all of these to become an entrepreneur, but they do need some. There are four types of productive resources: resources, human resources, capital resources, and entrepreneurship.

Resources are all the ingredients used to make the product. **Human resources** are the people who work to produce the goods. **Capital resources** are the things producers own, like inventory and tools. These are essential parts of making the goods we want and need. **Entrepreneurship** is when people use productive resources to produce a good or service to make a profit. A **profit** is the money left over after an entrepreneur pays for the resources it takes to produce a good or service. Entrepreneurship is a resource because even people who have access to other productive resources don't always start businesses.

Starting a business is risky. There is no guarantee consumers will want and buy what you produce. Entrepreneurs are willing to spend their own money on something that may or may not work out. Producers fail all the time. Sometimes, they are passionate about selling a product no one seems to want. They may have an excellent product that people would love, but they don't know how to let consumers know that the product exists. When a producer fails to reach consumers, they lose the money they spent to make their product. The **employees**, or people who work for the business, lose their jobs. Success in the marketplace looks amazing, but it comes with risks. Successful entrepreneurs have a talent for knowing what people need and want, how to gather the resources to make it, and how to advertise to consumers.

READ

Entrepreneurs Everywhere!

Have you ever heard of Elon Musk, the man behind Tesla vehicles? Musk is a very famous entrepreneur. He uses resources to produce goods that consumers want. He uses advanced technologies to create the vehicles of his dreams. Oprah Winfrey produces TV shows and magazines that consumers want to buy. She had a difficult childhood, but with hard work and natural talent, she has become one of the most successful entrepreneurs in the world. Steve Jobs, who made Apple products like the iPhone, was a famous entrepreneur.

Identify some real-life entrepreneurs. Name some who are famous and some who are not. Do you have any in your own neighborhood? If so, what do they do? Would you enjoy entrepreneurship? If you meet an entrepreneur, ask them how they knew their business would be successful.

Entrepreneurs, like the ones mentioned, are people who created something new and innovative, and became known worldwide. However, not all entrepreneurs are rich and famous. Entrepreneurs exist in every neighborhood and town. They can be people that start new businesses in a community. Maybe one of your neighbors started tutoring students in their home, and it grew into a business that now has its own store. Someone who enjoys baking may begin making treats, and that turns into a wedding cake business. These entrepreneurs may never be on the cover of magazines, or known by people around the world, but their contribution to the community is essential.

WRITE

What would happen if no one wanted to buy what an entrepreneur was selling? What are some reasons entrepreneurs fail? What is the difference between human capital and physical capital?

PRACTICE

Does the image show a human resource, a capital resource, or a basic resource that is an ingredient of a product? Circle the correct answer.

1. resource
   human resource
   capital resource

2. resource
   human resource
   capital resource

3. resource
   human resource
   capital resource

4. resource
   human resource
   capital resource

Circle the correct answer.

1. True or False   Only famous entrepreneurs affect communities.

2. True or False   Being an entrepreneur is risky.

3. True or False   Entrepreneurs are employees.

4. If a producer makes something that a consumer wants, what happens?

   A. The producer makes money.

   B. The producer loses money.

   C. The consumer is mad.

   D. The producer fails.

5. If a producer makes something that a consumer doesn't want, what happens?

   A. The producer keeps making it.

   B. The producer loses money.

   C. The consumer makes money.

   D. The consumer buys it.

6. Why should producers listen to consumers?

....

....

....

....

CREATE

Write a story about an entrepreneur who starts a business and gets very successful. You can choose what the person produces. The product or service should be part of the story. Make sure to talk about what the entrepreneur does to make the business a success.

7. What does it mean to sell something?

....
....
....
....

8. Define and give examples of these productive resources.

A. human resources

....
....
....

B. capital resources

....
....
....

C. entrepreneurship

....
....
....

Lesson 74

Saving

By the end of this lesson, you will be able to:

- define the importance of saving

Lesson Review

If you need to review the importance of entrepreneurs in a local community, please go to the lesson titled "Entrepreneurship."

Academic Vocabulary

Read the following vocabulary words and definitions. Look through the lesson. Can you find each vocabulary word? Underline the vocabulary word in your lesson. Write the page number of where you found each word in the blanks.

- **budget:** a plan for what to do with your money when you get it (page ____)
- **deadlines:** the dates by which you want to complete the things on a list (page ____)
- **financial goal:** choosing something to save up for (page ____)
- **flexible:** able to make changes (page ____)
- **income:** money that comes to you on a regular basis (page ____)
- **long-term saving:** putting away money for a long time, like for college (page ____)
- **short-term saving:** to save your money for a week or two to get enough to buy what you want (page ____)
- **short-term spending:** spend your money as soon as you get it (page ____)
- **strategy:** a plan of action made up of a list of tasks and deadlines for those tasks (page ____)

Do you have a piggy bank? How about a bank account? These are different ways you can save your money. You might be thinking that since you're a kid, you don't have much money and therefore have no reason to save it. But this is actually the best time to start saving! So get a piggy bank or find an envelope or wallet to start storing your money. Put it somewhere safe. This lesson will tell you all about the importance of saving.

What if someone told you that you could have anything you want—no matter the price? It probably sounds like make-believe, but there is a way! Many people tell you to save your money, but saving your money is a skill that can be learned. Furthermore, the earlier you learn this skill, the more money you will save!

Imagine you want a brand new bike that costs $200, but you don't have the money. Your friend's parents will pay you $20 a week to weed their garden. How long will it take you to have enough money to buy your bike?

....

Say you want a video game system that costs $90. You already have $40 saved. You start washing cars in your town for $10 a car. How many cars will you have to wash to buy your video game?

....

Saving for a Rainy Day

Have you ever heard the saying "saving for a rainy day"? This does not actually mean you should save money in case it rains. In this saying, a "rainy day" refers to saving money in case you fall upon hard times. If something breaks, it can be really hard to find the money to fix it. However, if you have savings, you can get the broken thing fixed without trouble.

READ

Why People Save

Once you start earning money, you should also start saving it. You've probably heard that it's important to save money, but do you know why?

Imagine you see a toy online. You want it, but it costs $50. A neighbor asks you to walk their dog every morning for $10 per week. After five weeks of walking the dog, if you save your money, you can buy the toy. After one week, you hear a noise. It's the ice cream truck. An ice cream cone would be nice. If you buy an ice cream cone for $4, you will need to wait an extra week to buy the toy.

Saving money isn't always easy, but it really pays off! You can do a few different things with your money. You can spend your money as soon as you get it, which is called **short-term spending**. You can save your money for a few weeks to save enough to buy what you want, which is called **short-term saving**. You can also put money away for a long time to save for big purchases, like college or a home, which is called **long-term saving**.

Having money come to you on a reliable basis, like being paid weekly, is called **income**. When you have income, you can **budget**, or plan, for what to do with your money. A budget makes your money more powerful. Before money arrives, you plan what is important to you and what you want to spend it on.

TAKE A CLOSER LOOK

Short and Long-Term Saving

There isn't a clear concrete difference between short-term saving and long-term saving. What might seem like a short time to one person could be a long time to someone else. However, generally speaking, short-term saving is for something you will buy in the next year. Long-term saving is for very, very expensive items like a car, house, or college. The good thing about long-term savings is that banks pay you if you let them store your money! This payment is called interest. It's not very much money, but it adds up over long periods.

READ

Making Financial Goals and Decisions

Making a budget isn't only about saving. With a good budget, you can put some money in savings and still have money for spending. Choosing something to save for is a **financial goal**.

If you ever saved your money to buy something, you have set a financial goal. To reach a goal, you need a plan. The best way to reach any kind of goal is to have a **strategy**, or a plan of action. A strategy should have a list of tasks and deadlines for those tasks. **Deadlines** are the dates by which you want to complete the things on your list.

Imagine you have decided to save $50 to give to a charity. Your first task might be to decide which charity you want to give the money to. Your next task could be to come up with a list of ways to earn extra money. You would also want to think about your deadline or how long it will take you to save $50.

It's important to stay focused on your plan. One way to stay focused is to find a picture of what you want to buy and hang it up where you can see it every day. Can you think of some other ways to stay focused?

Sometimes you need to be **flexible** or able to make changes to reach your goal. That way, if you run into a problem or something unexpected comes up, you can adjust your plan instead of giving up on it. Learning more about your goal can also be useful. If you watch the price and find a sale or coupon, you will need less money. If you read reviews of the toy, you may change your mind about how much you want it, depending on whether the reviews are good or bad.

Sometimes it's better to have one big, useful thing than a bunch of smaller, less useful things. For example, it's better to have a house than a bunch of toys. Part of growing up is learning how to say no to short-term spending so you can save for things you really want.

PRACTICE

Think of a financial goal you would like to reach. Then list three tasks you could do to start getting closer to the goal. Give each step a deadline. If you want more tasks, you can continue your plan on a new page.

MY FINANCIAL GOAL	
Tasks	**Deadlines**
1.	1.
2.	2.
3.	3.

What is something you could do to reach your financial goal faster?

....
....
....
....
....
....

REVIEW

In this lesson, you learned:

- Part of growing up is learning to earn and save money.
- Saving money is important because it's how we buy expensive things.
- Something we want but can't yet afford is called a financial goal.
- We can save for a short time or for a long time.
- We can reach a financial goal by using a budget.
- We should be smart about our financial goals.

Think About It

Starting a business is expensive. Business owners have to buy resources and pay employees. How do you think entrepreneurs get enough money to start a business?

Choose the correct answer.

1. Which of the following is an example of short-term spending?

   A. saving for a sailboat

   B. buying an ice cream cone

   C. getting your first car

   D. buying a diamond necklace

2. Which of the following is a short-term saving goal?

   A. a birthday present

   B. college tuition

   C. first house

   D. a trip to outer space

Use the words from the Word Bank to complete the sentences.

Word Bank: flexible   budget   income

3. Once you have a(n) _____, you should create a(n) _____ so you know what to do with your money. It's important to be _____ if you learn new information about your goal.

Do you have a savings account at a bank? Go to a bank in your town or online and start an account. You will need a grownup's help because bank accounts need to have an adult connected to them. You can start with change from your piggy bank, money from your birthday gifts, or money you made at your first job. Every time you get some money, put a portion in your savings account.

Answer the following question in complete sentences.

4. What is a financial goal?

....

....

....

....

....

Chapter 14 Review

By the end of this lesson, you will:

- review the information from the lessons in Chapter 14, "Income, Profit, and Wealth."

Lesson Review

Throughout the chapter, we have learned the following big ideas:

- People work to earn money so they can pay for goods and services they want and need. Many factors affect how much people earn at their jobs. (Lesson 71)
- Businesses are producers and customers are consumers. Producers create goods and services and consumers exchange money for them. (Lesson 72)
- Entrepreneurship is using resources to produce goods and services. There are famous entrepreneurs and everyday entrepreneurs in your neighborhood. (Lesson 73)
- Learning how to save money is important. It's how we buy expensive items. (Lesson 74)

Go back and review the lessons as needed while you complete the activities.

IN THE REAL WORLD

An average third grader sees about 300 advertisements a day. That's a lot of goods and services! You might not realize that advertisements are trying to get you interested in buying products. Look around your neighborhood, in your mail, and anywhere else you hang out. How many ads can you find?

REVIEW

People Power the Economy

You learned that businesses, customers, workers, and communities work together in an economy. People work so they can buy goods and services they want and need. Community members exchange goods and services to make sure everybody has what they need. All of this buying, selling, and working is known as trade. Workers trade their skills for money. The money we use to buy and sell is called currency. Sometimes people use credit cards and checks, but those things represent real money stored in banks. Banks hold money and move it around when we trade it.

Jobs have many different levels of income. How much money a person earns depends on factors like how good they are at their job and how valued their job is. Some occupations have vastly different wages, and it can be difficult to predict how much you will earn. It is important to consider different aspects when choosing your future career.

Producers are motivated to produce what they make by different things. Producers try to figure out what consumers want to buy so they can make a profit. Businesses have to compete with each other to get the consumers' attention. That is good for consumers because producers have to improve their offerings so we choose their product.

Having jobs allows people to focus on one skill, called specialization. People work because we depend on each other to keep our economy going. The economy provides many benefits.

Lemonade Producers

Both of these businesses are producers of lemonade. Which producer earns more money per day? Why? Compare and contrast these lemonade businesses.

WRITE Why might people who are offering a good or service need to hire employees?

....
....
....
....
....
....

REVIEW

Entrepreneurship

Businesses use resources to produce goods and services. Sometimes they hire people called employees to work in the business. Employees are human resources. Some people called entrepreneurs work for themselves. Their income comes from the profits they make from the goods and services they produce and sell. Being an entrepreneur is risky because there is no guarantee consumers will buy what you produce. Entrepreneurs spend their own money to produce something. When an entrepreneur fails, they lose the money they spent to produce their product.

Most people think of famous entrepreneurs, but entrepreneurs are everywhere. Anyone who uses their resources to earn a profit is an entrepreneur. Just as jobs have wage differences, earnings differ among entrepreneurs. Dog walkers and computer system designers earn very different incomes, but they are both entrepreneurs if they do not have a boss.

Having money come to you on a reliable basis is called income. Once you earn an income, you should start saving. We can choose what to do with our money. We can spend it on small things or save for a big purchase. The first step to saving is to create a financial goal and a budget. A budget is a plan for your money.

 Why does someone need to be a good saver to be an entrepreneur?

....
....
....

Compound Interest

You have probably heard that money grows when you save it. How can that be? Banks pay interest to people who store money at their bank. Your savings earns a small amount of money. You earn a little bit more each day. These are sometimes really small payments, only a few cents. However, over time, compound interest really adds up! Think of how much interest you can earn over the years if you put away some money now. Earning compound interest is a big incentive for keeping your money in a bank.

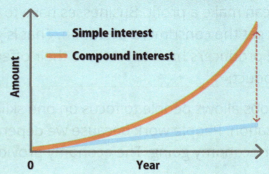

THE POWER OF COMPOUNDING
Compound interest VS Simple interest

PRACTICE

Missing Vocabulary

Use the Word Bank to fill in the missing words of the story.

Word Bank: entrepreneur   focused   deadline   want   desirable

financial goal   budget   services   income   need

advertisement   long-term savings   short-term spending

Luis wanted to buy a new video game, but it cost $125! Luis's parents said if he wanted to buy the game, he would have to earn the money.

"But I need it!" Luis argued.

"No, Luis. A video game is not a(n) _____. It is a(n) _____. You don't have to have it to survive. We need food, water, and shelter."

Luis wanted the game so much, but he thought about what his mom said. Every kid in the world wanted the game because it was so _____. The _____ listed all the features and made kids think they had to have it.

Luis came up with a plan. He set a(n) _____ of $125. He decided there would be no more _____ until he bought the game. Luis posted a sign on the telephone pole announcing that he was now a(n) _____. He would babysit, mow lawns, walk dogs, and other _____ too.

His first customer offered him $10 a week to walk his dog after school. Luis now had a(n) _____!

Luis created a(n) _____ to plan what to do with his money. He set a(n) _____ of one month to reach his goal. He posted a picture of the game on his fridge to stay _____.

It worked! Luis earned enough in his _____ to buy the game. Luis was so proud of himself, he decided to keep his job and start an account for college.

PRACTICE

Can You Be an Entrepreneur?

Entrepreneurs put their own money toward producing goods and services. They sell their products and pay their expenses. Any money they earn that is more than their expenses is profit. How much profit did these entrepreneurs make?

1. Sara opens a car-washing business. She buys $20 in supplies for her first day. She washes 10 cars and charges each car $10.

   A. What is Sara's profit? _____

   B. What kind of resources are Sara's cleaning supplies? Circle one:

      Capital resources   Human resources

2. Mason rakes leaves for his neighbors. It started with one neighbor but now does work for his whole neighborhood. Mason charges each homeowner $8 a week. He uses his parents' rake so he doesn't have to spend anything to run this business. Mason now has 8 customers.

   A. How much profit does Mason earn each week? _____

   B. The producer is _____ and the _____ are the neighbors.

3. Addison wants to raise money for a school fundraiser. She has started collecting aluminum cans from her recycling bin to take to the recycling center. Her neighbors decide to give her their cans too. She uses old trash bins to collect the cans so she spends nothing. In the end, she earns $123!

   A. What is Addison's profit? _____

   B. How does Addison's story show how we can use our money to help others?

   ....

   ....

   ....

REVIEW

Entrepreneurs don't get to keep all of the money that comes into their business because they need to pay for their productive resources. Entrepreneurs may have to pay for resources to make their products, human resources to create their products, or capital resources to help them manufacture the products. These are called expenses. An entrepreneur needs to pay expenses. Any money that is left over after the entrepreneur pays expenses is profit.

Discover! SOCIAL STUDIES • GRADE 3 • LESSON 75

PRACTICE

Desirable Goods and Services

Producers and entrepreneurs are always trying to figure out what consumers want and need. Match the good or service with the best time and place to sell it.

1. _____ American flags

2. _____ fresh turkeys

3. _____ sleds

4. _____ paper hearts

5. _____ sunscreen

6. _____ umbrellas

7. _____ raking leaves

A. Thanksgiving in America

B. Valentine's Day at card stores

C. a parade on Independence Day

D. winter in New York

E. a rainy day at a zoo

F. Fall in New England

G. Summer at the beach